Forming the Future
Is a Journey

Forming the Future Is a Journey

Frances Lorenz

Rev. date: 12/12/2019

To order additional copies of this book, contact:
Xlibris
1-888-795-4274
www.Xlibris.com
Orders@Xlibris.com
783696

Contents

Part III

The Spiritual Underpinnings

Part IV

Applications to the Future

Preface and Introduction

Forming the Future Is a Journey

Tell me, what is it you plan to do with your one wild and precious life?
—Mary Oliver

Somewhere in the mist of prehistory, our ancient ancestors created rituals around the bones of deceased tribe members and told stories about great battles and triumphs, and then—with ceremony, flowers, and other provisions—sent those persons forward into the mystery of the afterlife. They found solace in those stories we call myths, which are as old as the human race and alive in the foundational accounts of the life of Jesus and the tale of Buddha's enlightenment.

Myths, from the Greek *mythos,* meaning "word spoken with authority," show us what is important in the inner life. We each have a personal mythology that tells how life got to be the way it is for us.

Most myths can be condensed to a quest for the identification of the existential call, viewing it as a conflict of opposites and then finding a resolution that creates happiness. Just as the intellect solves problems in the physical world, myths are structured so that the mind can find meaning in and make sense of the world. *Forming the Future* is the name of a collective process I created to transform public education. It is also both my personal myth and revelation. It is the story of journeying through many dimensions of being and spiritual systems over a lifetime.

My thesis is that there is a direct relationship between our life journeys and Spirit. In the process of living our lives and evolving spiritually, we move through many dimensions of being. This inner journeying reflects in the world. Forming the Future implies an individual action that shapes the future. It contains the idea that an individual is not powerless to shape his or her own destiny. When I think of Forming the Future, I feel happy, and in saying those words, the mark is raised for all that is possible to achieve. As a mantra, it is a postulate in my consciousness for the magic that happens when spirit, soul, and body are in complete alignment. It is a remembrance of an experience of total surrender to something greater than myself.

Someone once commented that in leading many selfless projects over the years, everyone else had seemed to get a reward, but I had left myself out of the good that was available. Somehow I was not benefiting from what I was creating for others. I had to examine this. Was this true?

Later, a friend asked me, "Why don't you form your own future?" While it might seem odd, I have to say that my future has always formed me. There has been a spiritual calling and protection for my life that guided me to every job, to every experience. I have always been called into my work, from my first job in Head Start, offered by a friend in Del Valle, into my position of special assistant to the superintendent of schools in Austin, Texas. There I directed the multimillion-dollar Forming the Future program, which resulted in the restructuring of the school system, the passage of a $210-million bond issue, and the involvement of over twenty thousand people. Later, I was called by Al Mustin to my job as church administrator at the Church of Today, a Unity Church modeled after Jack Boland's church in Warren, Michigan, which initiated my path toward the ministry.

Given the way my life has unfolded, I know Spirit is forming my future. If my work is not satisfying, if I am no longer supposed to be there, I will be called to my next adventure. I have learned that in those few cases when I thought I myself was forming my future, Spirit had something else in mind. As a result, my life is very rich and fulfilling. I really do not want for anything. I would like to have a little more money for study and travel and remodeling the house, but beyond that I am happy watching people discover the God within themselves. That brings me deep joy.

In May of 1981, I was reading about the history of the Austin public schools and learned of an event held in Pease Park to celebrate the first year of its formation as a school district: parents, teachers, and administrators gathered together for a picnic in the park. What a great way to celebrate the centennial of Austin I.S.D. As I explored the idea further, it became apparent that Pease Park was too small to hold such a gathering. I was aware of school improvement projects, the reaction of parents to recent desegregation orders, and the need to unify the community toward a common good, what some call "spiritual democracy." An idea began to take shape. Why not find a way to bring together parents, teachers, and community leaders to work collaboratively in creating significant improvements in their schools, not only of facilities, but of the curriculum too? Little did I realize at the onset that I would be the one chosen to bring this project of spiritual democracy to fruition. The name "Forming the Future" was the invention of the new superintendent, and when he selected me to execute the project, neither of us suspected that it would have a life of its own.

As I revisited the project I will share in this book, I learned that Forming the Future was an allegory for my personal journey, my work in the community, and my spiritual revelation in the process. Hildegard of Bingen describes this work as a person becoming a flowering orchard: "[The Person] that does good work is indeed this orchard bearing good fruit . . . Whatever humanity does with its deeds in the right or left hand permeates the universe" (Fox, ed. 1983, 33).

Often our call in life presents itself metaphorically in symbols and repetitions, like motifs in symphonies. The metaphor of trees presents itself repeatedly in my spiritual formation: the tree of my childhood fantasy; the Kabbalah tree of life; the ceiba tree of the ancient Maya that grows down through nine dimensions and upward through thirteen; the Great Tree of Peace of our country's native ancestors, the Iroquois, that inspired unity and communication among six nations; the Celtic communion with trees, the deep roots of suffering; the roots of New Thought as a philosophy, a faith, a way of life that extends back thousands of years. All these trees create the flowering orchard Hildegard of Bingen envisioned and I aspire to become.

I was called into ministry in 1989. I attended Religious Science seminary and have served as a minister since 1994. Over the last twenty-five years, I have studied Creation Spirituality, integrating it into my own mystical tradition of Religious Science. About the time I initiated Forming the Future, I read Joseph Campbell's *Hero with a Thousand Faces*. I knew I was one of those faces on a sacred journey of learning about how I was rooted in God. For the first time I realized I was the heroine of my own life. This has evolved to an understanding that I am the heroine of God's life and that the Divine Feminine expresses through me.

My own spiritual journey places me clearly in the last third of my life, and I know that the choices I make now are important ones. Thomas Merton's advice that before doing anything we should consult our death makes sense today. The question I ask myself is "Does this project resonate so deeply within me that I want to expend a large part of what remains of my life's energy in dedication to it?" It seems there is less time available to experiment, but all the same I want to experience joy in living life to the full. Today I can say without a doubt that "God is," and I can also say that "I am." I know that God works in, through, and as me. That realization alone gives me deep fulfillment.

Most humans experience four distinct phases in the development of consciousness. At first, we feel a sense of victimhood, that we have been abandoned by or separated from God. Then seeking a way out of suffering, we learn some spiritual principles and tools, and develop enough self-confidence to work on the mastery of the material structures of life as Abraham Maslow describes in his hierarchy of needs: physiological: food, water, sleep, shelter, sex, homeostasis. Then we move to safety, love, self-esteem, and self-actualization where we experience fulfillment and happiness. In his later years, Maslow found another level he called transcendence. He equated this with the desire to reach the infinite. "Transcendence refers to the very highest and most inclusive or holistic levels of human consciousness, behaving and relating, as ends rather than means, to oneself, to significant others, to human beings in general, to other species, to nature, and to the cosmos" (Abraham Maslow, *Farther Reaches of Human Nature*, New York 1971, p. 269).

By mastering the stable structures in the physical realm, we are then able to embody a fuller understanding of universal principles on the cosmic level. We learn to surrender and let the divine move "through us" and then in its most mystical phase ultimately "as us."

It is in this servant consciousness that the mystical life is lived—after years of persistence, study, service, and meditation. Slowly, there is less reactivity, more forgiveness, and—ultimately—conscious oneness with the divine. It is a gentle knowingness that is graceful and in the flow. Recently, a friend came to mind in my meditation. She had gone to ministerial school in the early seventies, but when the school discovered she was African American, they would not let her live in the dormitory. She had left, with two other black students, deeply wounded by the experience. In my meditation, I saw her healed and returning to her original career choice. I had a clear revelation of her life. Later, she called me and said that she realized the only thing that mattered to her was living for God. She wanted to go dedicate her life to spiritual work. More and more, it is not *mythos* but revelation that is showing up in my life.

The awareness of God moving through us and as us is best gained in the silence and the pleroma or fullness of Spirit that is accessed in silence. In this book, I present how Spirit formed my future. There is a direct relationship between our life journeys and the development of consciousness. How do we speed up this growth? How do we awaken to our life's purpose? All the tools of spiritual practice—study of sacred texts, sermons, music, dance, chanting, ritual, meditation, and retreats— contribute to an enhanced awareness. As we live life more fully, we become more aware of many levels of consciousness, and with the expansion of consciousness, we discern that all things work together to create our future.

Consciousness converts possibility into actuality, which creates what we see manifested in our lives. Because my individuality is part of the whole, I, too, have causal potency that shows up in my creativity and acts of free will. When individuals take action in the world, they act with causal power. A greater future is only enhanced by union of the self with nondual consciousness.

When I was very young, I knew my purpose had something to do with communication and leadership. Sometimes side roads would attract me for one reason or another, but they did not work out because they did not lead to my soul's purpose. Today when opportunities do not come to fruition, I am grateful. I realize that Spirit is forming my future again. By adopting a position of nonresistance to whatever happens, I form my future and cocreate with Spirit.

Forming the Future placed me on a very large stage. I had to speak to audiences of hundreds of people about the future of the Austin public schools. But I had no inkling I was destined to become a minister until, after one of my speeches, an elementary school principal said, "Girl, you are a preacher!" In Forming the Future, I sent messages out to thousands of people with media appearances and large group presentations. The revelations I received about visionary leadership, faith, the magic of working with Spirit, using a beginner's mind, visioning, cocreation, detachment, trust, engagement, and choosing carefully are some of the topics developed in this book that emerged in developing the future as I saw it formed.

Just as I have used spiritual principles to inform my development of Forming the Future, I have applied these spiritual principles and archetypal patterns I derived from this project to my life. I hope my journey will inspire you to make a difference in your life. I hope you will believe it is possible to form the future of anything you care about. Most importantly, to become the change you wish to see in the world, forming the future of your own soul is essential. It is my pleasure to share my conviction that spiritual practice and democracy are essential components of the path to transcendence. It's my pleasure to share what I have learned with you.

Part I

The Past as Prologue

Chapter 1

The Hero's Journey: Forming the Future

Many of us are introduced to the hero's journey through the reading of fairy tales and myths and then discover its universality in our human experience: Medusas are slain, Minotaurs are found and killed, or Circe's spells are overcome. The journey represents a pattern of life, growth, and experience for all of us. We see it reflected everywhere: in television comedies, in the great works of literature, and in the paths our lives take.

Forming the Future involves discovering the patterns and determining which ones are life-affirming and which ones are no longer serving our greater well-being. Then as we uncover the unhealthy patterns, we may consciously choose to set our course in a new direction, making a subsequent journey armed with new spiritual tools. We are never at any point stuck, for, as Thomas Troward says, "Principle has no precedent" (Troward 1904, chapter 12).

We have learned that the three great aspects regarding subjective mind are its creative power, its amenableness to suggestion, and its inability to work by any other than the deductive method. Thus, by necessity, the Universal Mind must act deductively; that is, according to the law which has been found true of individual subjective mind. It is, thus, not bound by any precedent, which means that its creative power is absolutely unlimited;

since it is essentially subjective and not objective, it is entirely amenable to suggestion.

These discoveries throughout life are akin to journeys or rebirths. We are separated from the familiar and comfortable womb and initiated by the birth process into the world. Stanislav Grof studied NOSC (non-ordinary states of consciousness) induced by psychedelics and nondrug means such as holotropic breathwork. The focus of Grof's work has been pre- and perinatal periods as sources of psychological trauma. It is as Grof says:

> A radical transition from an aquatic form of life whose needs are being continually satisfied by placental circulation to the extreme emotional and physical stress of the birth struggle and then to a radically new existence as an air-breathing organism, is an event of paramount significance that reaches all the way to the cellular level. (Grof, 2007)

A birth trauma can color the entire life history of an individual. Indeed, the process of birth is a heroic journey in and of itself that can be normal or complicated. Much more is known in modern medicine about ways of alleviating birth trauma through creating more serene birth environments for mothers.

The cycle of the hero's journey repeats over and over again where old ways of thinking and acting are altered, opening the way to new levels of awareness, skill, and freedom. Each time the hero/heroine completes a cycle, she returns more confident, perceptive, and capable. Each challenge or change we face in life is a journey: every death, every love found, every love lost, every birth, each move to a new job, school, or city; every novel situation that confronts us or forces us to reevaluate our thinking, behavior, or perspective. Each journey functions as a holon in a holarchy, a series of nested experiences that are integrated and absorbed, each by the next. Sometimes confusing and painful, sometimes joy filled and blissful, the journey pattern helps us understand passages and progress in our lives.

Eight-Step Transformation

According to Joseph Campbell in *Hero with a Thousand Faces* (1949), the classic hero's journey has eight steps, but the sequence and number may vary from individual to individual.

Separation (from the known)
The Call
The Threshold (with guardians, helpers, and mentors)

Transformation
The Challenge
The Abyss
The Transformation
The Revelation
The Atonement

Return (to the known world)
The Return (with a Gift)

At its simplest level, the journey has three stages: separation, transformation, and return. On the purely physical plane of three dimensions, the hero's cycle is continuous.

First Stage: Separation

Our very birth separates us from the known womb into our new home that may or may not provide a warm and sustaining environment. It is in this waiting place that each us receives a call to adventure, to separate from home once more.

The Call invites a leave-taking and offers the chance to experience awe and gain something of spiritual value. Ernest Holmes says the Word is

> the ability of Spirit to declare itself into manifestation, into form. The Word of God means the Self-Contemplation of Spirit. The Manifest Universe as we see it as well as the

> Invisible Universe that must also exist is the result of the
> Self-Contemplation of God. "He spake and it was done."
> (Holmes 1926, 646)

It is the vision of Genesis that the creative energy of God spoke the sun and the moon, the light and the darkness, the vegetation and all the creatures into existence.

The element that the first cycle represents is earth. Earth or *humus* is the root word found in "humility." Humility does not mean submissiveness or unassertiveness. Fox defines it as being in touch with earthiness, with sensuality and passion, not as the repression of the creative power (Fox 1983, 59). We are drawn in by the divine to willingly undertake the quest, or—should we be too reluctant to change—we may be dragged in unwillingly.

The call may come during a crisis or a traumatic event in our lives. It can also appear as divine discontent or feeling out of sorts. Within this range the call can take many forms: a loss happens and we seek to reclaim what was lost, or we have an urge to explore the unknown, the allurement of the beautiful, the evolutionary impulse to seek greater complexity in our lives.

Once called to the adventure, the hero must pass over the threshold, the place where the known and the unknown meet. Often what pushes us over the threshold and into the unknown is an experience of loss or discontent: we sense something is missing in our lives, and we must search out what is missing; we want to save face or restore honor for ourselves or for a family member or for our community or country; we are rectifying a wrong, correcting an injustice, or fighting for human rights. Here we willingly cross the threshold into the watery recesses of our subjective mind to explore our divine depths. Holmes describes it this way:

> Within us, then, there is a creative field which we call
> subjective mind, and around us there is a field which we
> call Universal Subjectivity. One is Universal, the other
> individual, but in reality they are one. It is impossible to
> plumb the depths of the individual mind, because it is not
> really individual but individualized. Behind or within the

individualized point is the Universal which has no limits. In this concept alone lies the possibility of endless and eternal expansion. Everyone is Universal on the subjective side of life and individual only at the point of conscious perception. We use the power of the Universal Mind every time we think! (Holmes 1926, 93)

There are various kinds of thresholds: physical, emotional, mental, and spiritual. In myths, there are beings or situations at the threshold that block the hero's passage. These threshold guardians attempt to protect us from taking journeys for which we are unprepared. Once we demonstrate our readiness, they step aside. Usually, our parents function as our first threshold guardians. They try to keep us from doing things that would cause us harm. In adolescence, parents are challenged to both protect and encourage us to take on greater responsibilities as we get ready to live as independent adults away from home. In adulthood, the threshold guardians may morph from parental figures to formless fears, doubts, and ineffective behavior patterns. These false beliefs need to be laid to rest so we can develop our spiritual faculties.

There are thresholds into the physical outer world of action as well as thresholds into the inner world of thought and feeling. Often our exploration of the metaphysical occurs because of our encounter with a helper or teacher who provides assistance or spiritual direction. Sometimes they provide us with a talisman or divine gift that will help us through the work we must undertake. Their appearance at strategic times in our lives is what Jung calls "synchronicity."

The challenge is that every human being must take his or her own journey. Our helpers may guide and point the way, but they can't do the work for us. The challenge is ours, *must* be ours, if we are to benefit from it and grow.

Second Stage: Transformation

Once we enter the abyss, the place of emptiness, we experience that we have left home, our place of safety. Once past the threshold, we begin the journey into the unknown. The voyage can be one in which we empty ourselves and let go, or it can be a sharp encounter with pain and suffering. Sometimes we realize that our own willfulness is the challenge as we die to old patterns of behavior in our life in order to change and grow. Christians will recognize this threshold as the theology of the cross, of crucifying habits that no longer serve us. Crossing the threshold takes us into a confrontation with all the things we are afraid of: sex, grief, death, fear, anger, and especially the unknown. We are invited to learn to celebrate this place.

One of our greatest tests on the journey is learning how to tell the helpers from "tempters." Tempters try to pull us away from our path. They use fear, doubt, or distraction. They may pretend to be a friend or counselor in an effort to divert our energy to their own needs, uses, or beliefs. We must rely on our sense of purpose and judgment and the advice of our mentors to help us recognize true helpers.

Our challenges always seem to strike our greatest weakness: our shakiest emotion, our poorest skills, our most vulnerable state of mind. These challenges reflect needs and fears, and when we directly face them, we can incorporate and transform them from demons into angels. There is also the possibility that, because we are unprepared or have a flaw in our character, the challenge beats us or we cannot confront it. Then we may enter an abyss, and the adventure ends and we must return home again. But unless we make an attempt to take on our challenges, our life becomes a bitter shadow of what it could have been. We must "slay the dragon" of that something we dread or have repressed or need to resolve. Ernest Holmes describes repression as congestion within the mentality, which when bottled up secretes a poison in the system:

> People often become seething cauldrons within because of inhibited action. Energy must have an outlet. The solution of the problem of desire is to transmit any destructive tendency into some form of action which is constructive. However, an intellectual form of expression alone will not do this, for only those things to which we can give the complete self will solve the problem. (Holmes 1926, 628)

Holmes goes on to say that what we love will completely express the self and lose the energies of life into action and creative work. Often, allies appear to assist us in this work of mastering some new aspect of ourselves. They give us guidance, teachings, and spiritual direction.

The final step in the transformational process is a moment of death and rebirth: a part of us dies so that a new part can be born. Fear must die to make way for courage. Ignorance must die for the birth of enlightenment. Dependency and irresponsibility must die so that independence and power can grow. Part of the transformation process is a revelation, a sudden, dramatic change in the way we think or how we view life. This change in thinking is crucial because it makes us truly a different person.

Ernest Holmes defines revelation as follows:

> Becoming consciously aware of hidden things. Since the mind that man uses is the same Mind that God uses, the One and Only Mind, the avenues of revelation can never be closed . . . Eventually we shall know that the priceless revelation of "My Lord and My God" comes only when we turn to the Father within, Who has been there all the time awaiting our recognition . . . waiting to give us our revelation. (Holmes 1926, 630)

After we have been transformed, we go on to achieve atonement; that is, we are "at one" with our new self. We have incorporated the changes caused by the journey, and we are fully "reborn." In a spiritual sense, we are brought into harmony with life and the world. The imbalance that sent us on the journey has been corrected—until the next call. We have integrated the new status and identity.

The Third Stage: Return

After transformation and atonement, we face the final stage of our journey: our return to everyday life, to our home. Upon our return, we discover our gift, which has been bestowed upon us based on our new level of skill and awareness. We may become richer or stronger, we may become great leaders, or we may become enlightened spiritually. Our "home" may shift, too, with the new perceptions we have gained.

The essence of the return is to begin contributing to our society. In mythology, some heroes return to save or renew their community in some way. Other mythological heroes return to create a city, nation, or religion. Sometimes, however, things do not go smoothly. For example, we may return with a great spiritual message but find that our message is rejected. We may be ostracized or even killed for our ideal. We also run the risk of losing our new understanding, having it corrupted by putting ourselves back in the same situation or environment we left earlier. In some instances, the hero discovers she is surrounded by people whose level of understanding does not measure up to her new level of awareness. Frustrated, perhaps even lonely, she may go into exile to be on her own. Another great spiritual hero such as Buddha sacrificed the bliss of enlightenment to remain in the world and teach others.

Matthew Fox describes the hero's journey as a circle of four paths or *vias*:

> The four paths also address the question, Where will God, where will the experience of the divine be found in our time? Creation spirituality responds: the divine will be found in these places:
>
> In the Via Positiva, in the awe, wonder and mystery of nature, and of all beings, each of whom is a "word of God," a "mirror of God that glistens and glitters," as Hildegard of Bingen put it. This is Path One.
>
> In the Via Negativa, in darkness and nothingness, in the silence and emptying, in the letting go and letting be, and in the pain and suffering that constitute an equally real part of our spiritual journey. This is Path Two.
>
> In the Via Creativa, in our generativity we co-create with God; in our imaginative output, we trust our images

enough to birth them and ride them into existence. This is Path Three.

In the Via Transformativa, in the relief of suffering, in the combatting of injustice, in the struggle for homeostasis, for balance in society and history, and in the celebration that happens when persons struggling for justice and trying to live in mutuality come together to praise and give thanks for the gift of being together. This is Path Four. (Fox 1991, 18)

The four *vias* make a tree of life, representing new spiritual dimensions. It represents a hero's journey of endless growth through experience and aesthetic enrichment.

In forming my own future, I believe my purpose in the planet is to be a world server, and as I came to know truly, my mission was to save the positive thought. With millions of people focusing on the Apocalypse, I sometimes think saving the positive thought is a daunting task. But spiritual thought surpasses negative thought. Religious Science has adopted an expansive vision with which my heart resonates:

We envision the emergence of the Global Heart to balance and guide the further evolution of humanity.

We see a world free of homelessness, violence, war, hunger, separation and disenfranchisement.

We see a world in which there is a generous and continuous sharing of heart and resources . . . a world in which forgiveness, whether for errors, injustices or debts is the norm . . . a world which has renewed its emphasis on beauty, nature and love through a resurgence of creativity, art and aesthetics . . . a world in which fellowship prospers and connects through the guidance of spiritual wisdom and experience . . . a world in which we live and grow as One Human Family.

The United Church of Religious Science is a global community of people pervasively caring for and about each other and the entire human family, thereby bringing the gift of active compassion to the world. Our communities become "points of inspiration and influence," effectively advancing the vision of Global Heart. (http://*www.religiousscience.org n.d.*)

My work as a Centers for Spiritual Living minister embraces this vision. My study of Creation Spirituality has helped me embrace a new spiritual paradigm. The broad context of wisdom embraced by Wisdom University is along the lines of the Native American peoples' definition of wisdom: that the people may live. I have embraced the idea that Creation Spirituality is a spirituality that embraces social justice. Carl Jung observed, "All of the greatest and most important problems of life are fundamentally insoluble . . . They can never be solved, but only outgrown. This 'outgrowing' proved on further investigation to require a new level of consciousness" (Jacobi, ed. 1978, 304).

Acquiring a new level of consciousness is a continuing journey. It is an ongoing quest to find greater unity with the Whole. Our only knowledge of God must come through our own conscious awareness. I have come home to a new realization about my own connection to a long trajectory of many Creation Spirituality mystics. Mohandas Gandhi said, "You must be the change you wish to see in the world." Like produces like, attracts like, and creates like.

I talk to many community leaders about their disappointment in not being heard by elected officials in settings that are designed for citizen input. The will of the people is thwarted. I think of Forming the Future as a model of listening leadership. It is a way to synthesize and utilize public wisdom.

In Tibet, a story is told of a legendary kingdom that is a source of learning and wisdom, peace and prosperity. It is governed by wise and compassionate rulers, and the citizens are equally kind and learned. The place is called Shambhala. It is a spiritual society where all the people practice meditation and a path of loving-kindness. Some say Shambhala exists still, hidden in a remote valley somewhere. Others say the community disappeared and was elevated to some other heavenly plane. As a vision for community, I am attracted to that ancient kingdom. It represents what I seek for myself in community and is the foundation for Forming the Future.

Forming the Future was a process for listening to the community and elected officials and staff acting on recommendations for the future.

Chapter 2

The Heroine Is Called

In effect, if we can see the path ahead laid out for us, there is a good chance it is not our path; it is probably someone else's we have substituted for our own. Our own path must be deciphered every step of the way. There is surely a place for the strategic mind, the ability to plan, that lays out our every step in advance, but its ability to pay the monthly bills . . . can become an end in itself. What would it be like to link these powers of calculation and strategy with a radical embrace of the creative unknown, to put strategy in the service of the soul?
—David Whyte, *The Heart Aroused*

The call to community came when I was three years old and led a small band of neighborhood children into an excavation pit where the basement of a new home was being constructed. I did not like staying in my own home because it was far too restrictive for me. The house was shrouded in a pallor of death. When, a few years earlier, my mother had suffered the loss of her first child, Nancy, she was catapulted into a world of sorrow and she lost her mothering skills. She became inaccessible. I recall that nothing could get her attention. The loss of my sister happened when I had just turned one. Two years later she had another girl, and then her life became devoted to the new baby and neglecting me. I sought out friendship and camaraderie in the neighborhood, and found it.

That particular sunny summer day I had persuaded children—both older and younger than I was—that jumping into the pit was a worthy adventure. Suddenly, as I faced a six-foot wall of dirt, I had a sinking feeling we would not be able to get out again by ourselves. We needed help. I commanded two quivering children who had been afraid to jump to go tell their mother where we were and to come get us out. They didn't have to act, however, because moments later we were rescued by the bulldozer driver who lifted us out to safety.

I learned on that auspicious afternoon that leadership involves both risk-taking and the protection and care of followers. My old identity as an escapee from home out for adventure was stripped away by this falling-into-the-hole experience. I was not invincible but vulnerable. I was ashamed of my careless leadership. I was initiated into a new level of what it means to lead. But it took many years to integrate that new identity.

The experience awakened my mind to the larger context. It was a lesson in perspective too. In my small world, where I was trapped in the hole, I could only see a wall of dirt, much like the prisoners in Plato's metaphor of the cave who saw only the shadows and not the light. Had I turned ever so slightly, my perspective would have changed, because I would have seen that the pit sloped up to ground level at the back of the lot, and all of us could have walked out without any assistance. Shifting perspective and using the law of opposites has been a central spiritual practice of my life. The law of opposites, or polarity, holds that everything exists on a continuum. To counter a negative effect, one needs to focus on the opposite state of mind to reverse that condition.

When I was a child, no one ever talked to me about death or loss. My father never spoke of Nancy's death, but each year in August, when Nancy's birthday came around, my mother would cry and mourn. She would say that Nancy would have been seven or eight or nine. I could not figure out what had happened to my sister. Perhaps I had done something. I turned blame inward upon myself and felt powerless to make things better.

The theft of joy caused by the death of my sister compelled me to leave home. I discovered allies in older children and found friends who taught me significant things such as how to tie my shoe and the meaning of my name. Maya Angelou calls these significant others "rainbows in the clouds," individuals who unwittingly, by simple actions, lift us up and change our lives (Lecture at Evergreen University, Olympia, WA, February 17, 2007).

One ally, named Jeff, dubbed me "Frances San Francisco Carolyn South Carolina Bingham Bing Crosby Ham Plain Ham." It is an interesting naming. It contains a Franciscan monk who has inspired me; my favorite US city; the state of origin many of my ancestors; a singer, representing my talent for singing; and Ham Plain Ham, symbolizing my love of humor. Thus I learned that the community was a safe and friendly place, and discovered something about how to lead others. I learned that I had leadership skills and that with those skills came an awesome responsibility.

My world soon changed: my parents decided to move from South Bend, Indiana, to Texas. I was four years old. It was a departure that took them away from the memories of their loss. But the move also took them away from their circle of friends and me away from my community. It felt like a theft of all that I had built for myself. The new environment was hot and had strange insects such as chiggers and cockroaches, and three types of poisonous snakes. My mother stayed home while my father traveled as a salesman. My mother had taken a teacher's exam when she was thirteen and began teaching high school English early in life. By the time she married my father, she had almost twenty years' teaching experience. She decided it was time to take a break and stayed home to take care of my sister and me.

Despite the new environment, I made friends in the neighborhood once again, meeting an older boy who introduced me to magic tricks. We would ride the bus downtown to a magic store where we bought numerous tricks we used to play pranks on his older sister and my mother. I was also an avid reader. Not only did I read the many volumes my English-teacher mother had in her personal library, but also I made weekly trips to the library and polished off twenty books a day. It was a time of intellectual growth and intense creativity.

One of my favorite books is **Catcher in the Rye** (I loved J. D. Salinger's work). The title of the book comes from a song by Robert Burns. In chapter 22, his smart kid sister, Phoebe, asks Holden Caulfield what he wants to do with his life. Holden pictures himself in a rye field full of romping little children, standing at the edge of a cliff and catching the children before they run over the edge.

Phoebe points out that Holden has misheard the lyrics. He thinks the line is "If a body *catch* a body comin' through the rye," but the actual lyrics are "If a body *meet* a body, comin' through the rye," posing the question whether it is wrong for two people to have a romantic encounter, away from the public eye, if they do not plan any formal commitment to one another.

Some critics interpret Holden's stance to mean that he wants to catch the children before they fall out of innocence. For me, it seemed an image of protecting the good and beautiful in ourselves and in the world. I interpret Holden's metaphor to illustrate that we have spiritual power, which we can use either to destroy or to save. The curse and the blessing are one and the same thing, the power of mind used either negatively or affirmatively, the word used in fear and doubt or in hope and assurance. I believe Holden, in spite of his mixed-up psyche, did something profoundly sacred in declaring himself to be a "catcher in the rye." In a sense, he understood there is no greater authority than one's own soul.

Dare to take a stand for good. I like to think of this as my call to community, which began with my organizing the neighborhood children when I was three years old in my South Bend, Indiana, community.

Indeed, in Texas, I also was the defender of the neighborhood. I defended others and myself against bullies and instructed my friends how to defeat "Edward," a neighborhood terrorist. Edward would casually come from many blocks away and move systematically through the neighborhood, punching any child that crossed his path in the stomach.

When I told my father about the invader, he gave me my first instruction in self-defense: a boxing lesson. One day, when Edward walked up to me and punched me viciously in the stomach, I hauled back in perfect boxing form and hit him in the mouth. He bled a little and let out a yelp and ran home, never to return again to our neighborhood. I gave boxing lessons to the other children on our block, just in case Edward decided to come back. I must have been about eight years old.

Outdoors, my favorite thing to do was to climb the redbud tree in our backyard and imagine I was a messenger sending messages out into the world. I would wrap these imaginary epistles in the redbud leaves, roll them up tightly, and cast them into the air from my perch. When I was not sending out imaginary messages, I was building cardboard houses with secret chambers and inventing stories about the people who lived there, figures I had cut from old Simplicity pattern books the neighborhood store had discarded. Using these cut-out characters, I made up stories for any children who gathered around me to listen.

I became a skilled storyteller, entertaining friends at school under a large oak tree. I remember more than a dozen children would gather to listen to the stories I made up on the spot. It became a truly artistic period in my life when I discovered I could paint and draw too. My father, an artist, encouraged this gift. My mother sought to have a concert pianist in the family and arranged for me to have piano lessons each week. I was transformed into a fairly confident artist, writer, singer, musician, and storyteller.

I was called to spiritual pursuits when I was twelve, and my mother shared Ernest Holmes's *The Science of Mind* with me. I avidly read through its hundreds of pages. Its inclusive philosophy, faith, and way of life spoke to me deeply. One of the most exciting chapters was "The Law of Attraction."

Taking as the starting point the idea that the essence of man's life is God, it follows that he uses the same creative process. Everything originates in the One comes from the same Source and returns again to It. As God's thought makes worlds and peoples them with living things, so our thought makes our world and peoples it with our experiences. By the activity of our thought, things come into our life and we are limited only because we have not known the Truth. We have thought that outside things controlled us, when all the time we have had that within which could have changed everything and given us freedom from bondage.

Everyone automatically attracts to himself just what he is, and we may set it down that wherever we are, however intolerable the situation may be, we are just where we belong. There is no power in the universe but ourselves that can free us. Someone may help us on the road to realization but substantiality and permanence can come only through the consciousness of our own life and thought. Man must bring himself to the place in mind where there is no misfortune, no calamity, no accident, no trouble, no confusion, where there is nothing but plenty, peace, power, Life and Truth. He should definitely daily using his own name declare the Truth about himself, realizing that he is reflecting his statements into Consciousness, and they will be operated upon it.

In mysticism this is called High Invocation; invoking the Divine Mind, implanting within It, seeds of thought relative to oneself. This is why some of the teachers of olden times used to instruct their pupils to cross their hands over their chests and say: "Wonderful, wonderful, wonderful me!" definitely teaching them that as they mentally held themselves, so they would be held, "Act as though I am and I will be." (Holmes 1926, 294–5)

The words of this text fell on my soul like manna. The law of attraction was brought to our national attention in 2007 in a film called *The Secret* and was discussed on the Oprah show. I was excited to come in touch with this law many decades ago. I savored the meditations for self-help that Holmes wrote:

I shall keep the promise that I have made to myself.

I shall never again tell myself that I am poor, sick, weak nor unhappy.

I shall not lie to myself any more, but shall daily speak the truth to my inner Soul, telling It that It is wonderful and marvelous, that It is One with the Great Cause of all Life, Truth, Power, and Action.

I shall whisper these things into my Soul until it breaks forth into songs of joy with the realization of Its Limitless possibilities.

I shall assure my Soul. (Ibid., 517)

Right after reading the text *The Science of Mind* on a warm Saturday morning in May, I woke up and scrambled downstairs. It was a happy time for me. I was doing well in school and had many friends in the neighborhood. The sadness of my early childhood years had been resolved. My mother was present again; my father was happy in his creative work in sales. We had just moved from east Dallas to a Tudor-style home in University Park, Dallas. My parents told me they were going to run to the grocery store with my sister and would be back in half an hour. As they backed the car out of the driveway, I stood in the doorway of my parents' bedroom and had an enormous experience of spiritual energy. My life was never the same after that moment.

Almost immediately I felt what is sometimes referred to as a "quickening" of consciousness. Any influx of energy, whether it is chemical, electrical, or personal, produces change. I believe the levitation experience opened me to an enormous influx of energy, which produced in me a greater awareness of being an integral part of an infinite and timeless continuum.

I became intensely interested in religion and philosophy. On weekends, I would take the bus to the downtown Dallas public library and spend hours in the religion and philosophy sections. I was reading books that compared the Bhagavad Gita to the Bible and noted that the Golden Rule was the singular thread in all religions. I was compelled to write plays about faith healers, along with mysteries that entertained my classmates at school. My best friend, Mimi, was the daughter of the pastor of the second-largest Baptist church in Dallas. I visited her church but could never understand the concept of "being saved."

Neither did I feel at home in the Episcopalian church. I was constantly feeling faint in the service, and my father would walk me out to the fresh air. We attended the Episcopalian church of my father's tradition. My mother had become enamored of metaphysical spiritual teachings. She shared with me her Rosicrucian experiments in which she had an out-of-body experience. She also told me that one day, after Nancy's death, when she was lying down on the couch in the living room, the whole room had filled with light, and Jesus had appeared surrounded by little children. She had thought, "I wonder if Nancy is there," upon which the whole vision shattered and disappeared. Ordinary denominational religion seemed tame in comparison to the instruction I was receiving from my mother and my own mystical experiences.

After my vibrational experience, almost anything I wanted to learn became readily available to me. My mother loved to read, and one day she shared her latest book with me, *The Search for Bridey Murphy* by Morey Bernstein. In 1952, Bernstein, a therapist, put Virginia Tighe into a hypnotic trance and regressed her to a past life. Virginia was the wife of a businessman in Pueblo, Colorado. While under hypnosis, she told Bernstein that more than one hundred years earlier she was an Irish woman named Bridget Murphy who went by the nickname of Bridey. During their sessions together, Bernstein held detailed conversations with Bridey, who, with a pronounced Irish brogue, spoke extensively of her life in nineteenth-century Ireland. When *The Search for Bridey Murphy* was published in 1956, it became a bestseller and sparked worldwide interest in the possibility of reincarnation.

The facts were investigated, and much of what Bridey said was consistent with the time and place. But no one could find a historical record of Bridey Murphy—not of her birth, her family, her marriage, or her death. Believers supposed that this was merely due to the poor record keeping of the time. Critics learned that Virginia had grown up near an Irish woman named Bridle Corkell, whom she had known well and who could have been the inspiration for "Bridey Murphy." Nevertheless, the case of Bridey Murphy is a thought-provoking story. I was fascinated with hypnosis and taught myself how to do it by checking out books from the library on medical hypnosis. I learned that the mind is capable of creating many things and can receive and act upon suggestions at both a conscious and unconscious level.

I went to college and enrolled in a fine arts program, which I later abandoned for an English- and Spanish-degree program. Having drifted away from my goal of becoming an artist, I moved into a career in education almost as an afterthought in my early twenties. I served as a teacher, principal, and program director, and finally as assistant to the superintendent for Forming the Future.

My first job offer was from a new Head Start program in the Del Valle Independent School District. A visiting teacher and friend was recruiting part-time teachers. The next year, I learned about the Creedmoor Bilingual

School, an experimental school designed by Dr. Theodore Anderson. I applied and became the fifth-grade teacher and assumed some duties of the visiting teacher. The following year the principal left the program and recommended me. I became principal of the school. In the ensuing years, the school received the Tri-State Award for best elementary school. It was expanded to include K-5 and a junior high program 6–8. Then I was recruited by my former Del Valle superintendent to direct a new million-dollar Communication Skills Program. It was funded through Title II, Model Cities, and the Austin Independent School District. It had a parental involvement component, which I named "Happy Talk" that was based on development of verbal interactive skills through the research of Denise Levertov. When that program ended after three years, I was offered a position in the department of developmental programs that did experimental research projects and grants for the school district's education programs.

In the summer of 1981, I was contracted to direct Forming the Future. The project ended in 1983 with the successful passage of a bond issue with 4–1 margins.

In his book *The Great Work* (1999), Thomas Berry poses the question "What now is my great work?" as an invitation to consider how all of us can work more effectively to take care of our planet. When the Forming the Future project was over, I felt deflated. It was as if my life had no meaning or significance, as if I had reached some sort of pinnacle beyond which there was no future. Then one day, I had a profound waking dream in which a beautiful raven-haired woman bent down and whispered in my ear, "You haven't even begun to do the work you'll do." This messenger guaranteed success. And yet, to my knowledge, that promise is still to be manifested. I still do not feel I have surpassed the work I did in Forming the Future.

> *It may be when we no longer know what to do,*
> *we have come to our real work,*
> *and that when we no longer know which way to go,*
> *we have begun our real journey.*
>
> —Wendell Berry

This is where I find myself today: just beginning the real journey and exploring what is in store for me in the future.

The following three chapters introduce the three mentors who had a significant influence upon my worldview: Ernest Holmes, the founder of Religious Science; Matthew Fox, the author and founder of Creation Spirituality; and Paula Underwood Spencer, who taught me about Native American spirituality and wisdom.

If you asked Ernest Holmes if he was Christian, he would answer yes. But his is an entirely different form of Christianity than is seen in most churches. New Thought embraces the teaching of Jesus as well as the goal of attaining Christ consciousness. It rejects fear-based religion with a punitive, all-controlling Father God. Holmes drew from the wisdom of the world's spiritual traditions as well as Jesus's teachings to establish the diversity and universality of spiritual principles.

Fox likewise has instituted a reconstruction of modern-day Christianity and in 2005 posted ninety-five theses or articles of faith for Christianity for the Third Millennium on the door of the same church where Martin Luther had posted his. Fox's twenty-five years of reform have contributed greatly to my being able to retrieve my religious roots and accept them. He has given me a new way to be "Christian" and yet not conform to the structure that exists today in the traditional church.

Paula's work gave our nation's ancestry a new meaning and purpose. I am still seeking information to document the family story of my Native American great-great-grandmother.

Chapter 3

Forming the Future with Ernest Holmes, Creation Spirituality Mystic

From a young age, I have embraced the philosophy, faith, and way of life Dr. Ernest Holmes espoused and described in *The Science of Mind*. Matthew Fox called Ernest Holmes a *creation spirituality mystic* (Fox, 2004). One of the ten core concepts of Science of Mind is wholeness. Wholeness, Spirit is a transcendent, perfect whole that contains and embraces all seeming opposites. As human beings, we have free will and can choose what we experience, whether it be positive or negative. The same principle that brings us freedom, prosperity, and joy also allows us to experience bondage, lack, or misery, according to our consciousness.

This evolutionary concept of wholeness says that all seeming opposites can be embraced. Higher wholeness can be referred to as God. In a nonreligious context it can be referred to as nondualistic or both/and thinking. Typically, institutions desiring to learn the will of the community gather safe, friendly individuals to participate. This practice limits the fields of possibilities represented by a diverse body of participants.

> We believe that the Universal Spirit, which is God,
> operates through a Universal Mind, which is the Law of

God; and that we are surrounded by this Creative Mind which receives the direct impress of our thought and acts upon I understand that OUR LIFE is God. (Holmes, on religiousscience.org)

Holmes said this philosophy should be open at the top, open to new revelation, and he would be very surprised if people were still reading his textbook twenty-five years hence. The fact that his writings are still being read attests to the wisdom of Creation Spirituality and his understanding of universal spiritual principles. Were Holmes alive today, he would be incorporating concepts from new physics into his work. He said, "We are changed from glory to glory" (Holmes 1926, 490). He affirmed evolution in consciousness and that we are on an ascending scale of life. There is no end to Spirit and our possibility of expressing it, but we have to image it in our own minds.

> The world is saturated with Divinity, immersed in Reality, and filled with possibility. We must take this divine possibility and mold it into a present actuality in everyday experience This is the way to freedom, the pathway to peace and happiness. (Ibid., 490)

Holmes connected creativity to Spirit: "We do affirm the Spirit as transcendent, having the ability to create new thoughts while new thoughts create new situations" (Ibid., 321). When we use the laws wrongly, we impose suffering upon ourselves and others. We have free will to use the laws for good or for ill. Fox notes this about Holmes: "[His] spiritual genius is on a parallel with great creation mystics of the past, from Jesus to Hildegard to Aquinas to Eckhart to Julian of Norwich and more. We are blessed to be drinking from his wisdom today, and today that wisdom is needed more than ever" (Fox 2004).

While studying the writings of Ernest Holmes, I became aware that my thoughts have built my reality. Louise Hay, a practitioner of Religious Science and author of *You Can Heal Your Life*, says she cured herself of cancer by changing her mental patterning. What continues to be intimated to me is that my mind interacts with a Universal Mind or participates in a

Cosmic Reality Principle. We are bound or freed by how we choose to use our minds. The future is shaped by how we choose to reinvent a world on fire and how we protect all that is good and beautiful in ourselves, in our special relationships, and in the world. It is this reinvention that can take place when sufficient participation from the community is enlisted.

Holmes says that we must take the principle of life and apply it:

> We have discovered . . . that we live and have our being in what we call an infinite Mind, an infinite creative Mind, an infinite receptive Mind, an all-operative Mind, an omnipotent Mind, an all-knowing Mind. And we have learned that that Mind presses against us on all sides; it flows through us. It becomes operative through our thinking. (Holmes 2001, 74)

When I receive a revelation in meditation that I can do something, I have to do it to prove I have the revelation. Many people I know tell me of revelations they have received from Spirit and are content to keep telling the story of their revelation without taking any concrete action in the world. This is not what is intended. How else can Spirit operate in the world but through its manifest creation in nature and in human beings? I am one with an Infinite Intelligence that makes things out of itself. Life operates for me by flowing through me. We live in consciousness, not in the conditions of life. The more I seek a goal that aligns with the principle of the unfoldment of life and love, the more support I will have from Spirit. I have learned that the more my personal goal is of benefit to other people, the more likely it is to succeed. It is about entering into a greater consciousness about everything.

How do I activate this? It is done through the Word, the logos or living word operating through me. The activity of Spirit within me is creative. The power of my word creates activity. As I feel a greater sense of communion with the Universal Spirit, God within me, God everywhere present, I am connecting with a larger field of intelligence that resonates with me. Spirit does the rest. I can use the Word to deny false appearances and affirm the truth even though it appears real. I can speak my word for my business, church, family, health. As I hold the perfect vision, I enlarge my consciousness until it realizes all good. I am sowing a seed into the universal mind of the Absolute. I am forming the future.

At a very young age, I realized that if I wanted to create a definite manifestation, I must produce a definite inner activity. It is not about dealing with outer conditions but with mental and spiritual law. The more I embrace the power of thought and spiritualize it, the higher will the manifestation be that I create. The more I rely upon Spirit, the greater the outcome. I learned that if I thought about learning something or executing a project and could hold the vision clearly in mind and then act upon it, there would be a successful outcome. I had the impression of being in touch with some field or intelligence larger than myself that was even lending me assistance in its execution. Somehow, my personal volition intersected a larger whole that supported me.

Ernest Holmes emphasized that the goal for every individual is the complete emancipation from discord of any kind. This entails mastery over the words we speak and over the thoughts and feelings that form the creative word. It is easy to become distracted by pessimism, chaos, and negativity. The truth is that life is ready to give to us all that it has. Everything depends upon our consciousness. "So as he thinketh in his heart, so is he" (Prov. 23:7). Jesus taught nothing else. He said, "The words which I speak unto you, they are Spirit, and they are life" (John 6:63b).

God governs the universe through spiritual laws that work out the divine will and purpose, always operating from Intelligence. We live in an intelligent universe. This Intelligence is so vast and its power so great that our human minds cannot grasp it; all that we can hope to do is to learn something of the way it works and to harmonize ourselves with it, so we can align ourselves with Spirit and obtain harmony in our lives.

The Word is a principle that can be proven. We know Mind exists and that it will correspond to our thinking about it. This is the reason Jesus said, "It is done unto you as you believe." There is *something* that does it, which never fails. We must believe that our word is formed upon and around this Creative Mind.

For instance, if we want to create activity in a project, we must believe our word is law about that thing, and that there is *something* that takes our thought and enhances it, bringing it into manifestation. Our word is what determines what will manifest on the physical plane. The mind is so malleable that the slightest thought makes an impression upon it. Indecisive people can expect to receive confused manifestations in their lives. If a gardener plants a hundred different seeds, he is likely to get a hundred different plants. It is the same with Mind.

Ernest Holmes affirms that the Word of God is the power of Spirit to declare itself into manifestation. The manifest universe is the result of the self-contemplation of God. The Word is the image, idea, or thought of God speaking itself into manifestation. It is what sets power in motion. There is only One Life, Mind, and Spirit. "When our word is spoken in this consciousness of life, power and action, then our word *is* life, power and action" (Holmes 1926, 475).

No one believed that Forming the Future was possible. Several attempts to call citizen planning groups together had failed. The greater our conviction and the bigger our consciousness, the more power our thoughts will have. For a while, at the beginning of Forming the Future, I thought that the superintendent and me were the only ones who believed it was possible.

Chapter 4

Worldviews and Creation Spirituality

Throughout history, two basic worldviews have emerged: one that humanity is not capable of governing itself and should be controlled by an educated elite, and the second that humanity is inherently good and capable of participating in its own governance. Beyond these worldviews is an essential theology about the nature of human beings and the nature of God. One of the teachings I embrace through my understanding of Ernest Holmes is that human beings are microcosms of a benevolent God. Since God is inherently good, human beings are also inherently good.

My first exposure to the writings of Matthew Fox came through reading *On Becoming a Musical, Mystical Bear: Spirituality American Style*, published in 1972. I discovered this book in 1976. The thrust of this book is toward a creation-centered or life-affirming spirituality. Before reading Fox, I had never known that mysticism could be tied to prophecy or that prophecy was a call to make the world a better place. The relationship between justice and spirituality was unclear to me until I read Matthew Fox.

Fox suggests that the idea of love varies with cultural circumstances. "Does love have a name today?" he asks rhetorically and answers,

> I suggest that love today means before all else justice.
> Justice is the direction given to love. For the only way
> to love God is by loving one's neighbor, but the only way
> to love one's neighbor (apart from "being in love" which
> limits one's understanding of neighbor) is by justice. Very
> simply, he who says he loves his neighbor but ignores
> justice is a liar. And he who says he loves God whom he
> does not see, but hates his brother, whom he does see, is
> a liar . . . Justice is the first concern for those who love
> life, and he who prophesies that is speaks (i.e., acts) on
> behalf of the one who is Life who speaks in the Spirit and
> the Spirit in him, speaks against injustices, in particular
> against those enemies that rob others of their first gift: life.
> (Fox, *On Becoming A Musical, Mystical Bear*, 105–6)

Someone once said that every headline in the newspaper or online news streams is a request for prayer. Just what is meant by prayer? Working for justice involves a change in the self because we can only radically change our own life. The lives of others are altered through love, and even then it is up to each person to alter himself. This transformation into a prophet according to Fox (Ibid, pp. 109–115) has five aspects:

1. Rerooting oneself personally by enjoying life and becoming a radical lover of life.
2. Reluctance - Often a prophet will put savoring life ahead of fighting for it. The prophet is shy and reluctant to act and will engage only when the call becomes so strong it cannot be swept away.
3. Creativity - The response of a prophet creates and encourages creativity.
4. Community orientation - The prophet realizes at a subjective level prayer unites the entire community. Community is always becoming, which is building anew.
5. Price of prophecy - While many prophets suffer, it is not masochistic suffering. Prophets sustain a belief that life is a gift when appearances might dictate otherwise. They instill hope that

"evil will not triumph over good." Not a single person can enjoy life alone. It is always shared with others.

We find in today's world in which we are experiencing climate change that "community" can really only mean worldwide community. As we engage in reducing poverty, environmental destruction, disease, and ignorance, it must be for the entire human race. We have the creative power to make a difference. Prophets have a community orientation. We are all part of the One Mind, and at the level of the unconscious, we all share symbols and experiences in common. Community is always striving for what will form the future. The word *community* comes from the words *cum* and *munio*, meaning to "build with." Many prophets (Gandhi, King, and others) paid a price for their radical response to life, but their actions assure that human history will be changed forever.

Finally, Fox ends his book with the poem "On Becoming a Musical, Mystical Bear," the whimsical title that got my attention in the first place (Ibid.,117).

> Come on out to the countryside, out where our fathers died,
> Come on out, now take a ride,
> 'Cause there's somethin' to see—Gonna save your hide.
> There's a bear out there in the countryside,
> He prays where he stays and it ain't in his lair
> He's a musical, musical, mystical bear.
> Oh yeah! . . . a musical, mystical bear.

According to Fox, the bear represents a person who knows how to enjoy life without feeling guilty. The bear is preparing to stick out his chin for the sake of justice: "This tension is the substratum on which an adult creation-centered spirituality is based" (Ibid., xvii). Childish, otherworldly spirituality has not led to the correction of injustice.

Finally, Fox says, "Where one's capacity to become outraged at injustices is smothered and barely smolders, so does one's capacity for loving justice. It follows then that the development of the prophet in each of us waits for the development of the mystic in each of us. As we grow in our powers to love life we will advance our urge to share it and to wrestle with its enemies" (Ibid., 139). We must be concerned about our future.

Matthew Fox was a powerful influence upon my continuing passion for social justice. His philosophy set the stage for my involvement in Forming the Future.

Chapter 5

The Deep Democracy
of the Iroquois

When I was young, my aunt told me that my great-great-grandmother was Cherokee, and that after the Trail of Tears she had left her family to search for her people. Years later, I studied census data from 1840 that confirmed her absence. Only V. Jameson, head of household, with six children under the age of twelve, showed up at their Missouri homestead. I am still searching for evidence that will prove these relationships today. My daughter's DNA reveals the evidence of both North and South American indigenous people. It was fortuitous that I met Paula Spencer Underwood and heard her narratives of her book *The Walking People, a Native American Oral History*. I learned that the Cherokee were a branch of the Iroquois and had moved south from the state of New York into North Carolina. I have always been drawn to my native ancestors. For many years now, I have sought information about my great-great-grandmother.

I first met Paula Spencer Underwood in the late seventies. She was speaking at a local church in Austin and was sharing excerpts from her oral-tradition book, a learning story called *Who Speaks for Wolf?* (1983). At the time, I was working for the public schools in developmental programs, a department engaged in research and innovation. After her reading, I expressed an interest in piloting a program in the school district. I helped

Paula and her editor, Jeanne Slobod, make the necessary connections within the school system to put this program in place.

During that time, I had frequent meetings with Paula and Jeanne. We would sit in Jeanne's apartment in downtown Austin, and Paula would tell stories from her oral history. I learned about the deep democracy of Iroquois wisdom and how Iroquois leaders had met with the framers of the American constitution and shared their own very special constitution and methods of governance, a connection that had a major part in the shaping of the United States Constitution.

Jeanne Slobod was also funding the research of Dr. Donald Grinde, whose project synthesized all available documents surrounding the Iroquois–Founding Fathers connection. The constitution of the Iroquois confederacy is The Great Law of Peace, which was used by the Founding Fathers in drafting the United States Constitution. The unique inclusivity of The Great Law was that men and women shared equally in the leadership of their nation and all life was treated as sacred. Many historians believe that the US Constitution was influenced more by the Iroquois Great Law of Peace than by Greek democracy, as is commonly taught.

The Union of Nations was established prior to major European contact, complete with a constitution known as the Gayanashagowa (or "Great Law of Peace") with the help of a memory device in the form of special beads called wampum that have inherent spiritual value. Traditional anthropologists have speculated that this constitution was created between the middle 1400s and early 1600s, but the oral tradition suggests the federation was formed around August 31, 1142, based on a coinciding solar eclipse (Mann and Fields, 1997).

When the confederation of Iroquois Nations was formed, an evergreen tree was chosen to symbolize the living nature of the confederacy: the many needles represented the individuals of each nation, the bundles of needles were families, the twigs were clans, and the branches represented whole nations. The trunk of the Great Tree of Peace represented the confederacy and united earth and sky as two aspects of life that nourish human beings. From the Great Tree grew the four White Roots of Peace, representing the four directions.

The Five Nations each buried a war hatchet under these roots, vowing to never again fight each other. An eagle was placed on top of the tree to represent the high vision needed to see any changes coming so that the people could consult with each other and take effective action. All decisions were to be made in consideration of seven generations. How would an action affect the grandchildren's grandchildren? And after them, their children?

One of the stories Paula shared with us from her tradition was the Rule of Six. The Rule of Six says that for every apparent phenomenon, one must devise at least six plausible explanations. By devising at least six, we are sensitized to how many more there might be and keeps us from jumping to conclusions or locking on to the first thing that sounds right as "The Truth." When she was a child, Paula's father would have her stand on her left foot, and he would say, "Answer this question in the manner of the people." Wholeness. Then he would have her stand on her right foot, and he would say, "Explain this in a way your mother would understand." Sequence. Then he would have Paula stand on both feet, and he would ask, "What do you see now?" Paula learned that it wasn't enough to just do one or the other. A balance needed to be struck between the two. In this process of pedagogy, Paula learned to think for herself.

The Iroquois truly understood the confederated structure. It was the one Benjamin Franklin was familiar with and after which he modeled his Albany Plan of Union in 1754. This plan became the basis for the constitution of the colony (now *state*) of New York, from which the United States Articles of Confederation were taken. Though there is a definite line of transmission from the Iroquois document to our own constitution, the latter never measured up to the inclusive integrity of the Iroquois model: slaves were not freed, nor were women given the right to vote in the United States Constitution of 1776. In Paula's *Oral History*, the Iroquois who attended the 1776 convention left with sadness at the outcome.

Native Americans were considered citizens of foreign nations rather than citizens of the United States. They were often invisible, but Paula tells many stories that were passed down about the Oneida chief Skenandoah, who was born of Oneida parents at Conestoga, just downstream from Harrisburg. In the 1750s, he was sent as a delegate to find the Cherokee in the Appalachian Mountains and to discuss the problems of the French and Indian War. In 1754, he attended the Albany Treaty Conference, where Hendrick, a Mohawk chief, played a prominent role for the Iroquois.

Skenandoah is reported to have often visited at the home of Sir William Johnson, colonial statesman and friend of the Iroquois. Sir William established a council fire of the Six Nations and carried on his Indian diplomacy there. Paula's oral history says that in 1755 Benjamin Franklin asked Skenandoah to go to western Pennsylvania to help Lt. Col. George Washington by hunting for food for his men during Gen. Edward Braddock's campaign against the French.

During the thirty-year period preceding the Constitutional Convention (1787), the Iroquois assisted the colonists many times in their struggles against the French and other Indian tribes. Paula's *Oral History* says that Skenandoah was part of a delegation to the Constitutional Convention, and when the Iroquois were no longer useful to the colonists, they returned north. In 1777/78, the Oneida offered 250 warriors to the colonist cause, assisting George Washington's men with provisions of corn. Skenandoah continued to serve as a renowned Oneida elder well into the 1800s and died March 11, 1816. He had been a loyal ally of the colonies during the revolution.

How did this connection between the Iroquois Confederacy and Benjamin Franklin come into being? Benjamin Franklin started printing accounts of Indian treaty councils in his print shop in 1736, and for twenty-six years he continued to print the accounts of Indian treaty councils with the colonials until 1762 (Underwood 1997, 106). In 1744, Pennsylvania appointed Franklin to be the commissioner for Indian affairs, and in that position he learned how the various Iroquois nations negotiated trade and policy matters on an equal basis with the colonial governments. The councils were conducted on Indian terms, with exchanges of wampum belts and much oratory on all sides.

The *Oral History* describes a close relationship between Benjamin Franklin and the Iroquois. The Iroquois League was a well-organized alliance of five nations whose geographical territory ran from the St. Lawrence south into Pennsylvania and west to Illinois. It controlled both the Hudson-Mohawk and St. Lawrence valleys, and this alliance became the basis for state and federal forms of government.

Who Speaks for Wolf? is the learning story of a tribe that decides to move to a new location. Everyone gathers in tribal council and discusses the pros and cons of each of the choices for new locations. Finally, a site is selected. Unfortunately, the site is the home of a pack of wolves. At first, the tribe decides to share food with the wolves so that they will not raid the village. But as winter approaches, they cannot spare extra food to feed the wolves too. In the end, the relationship doesn't work out and the tribe has to move again. The question posed is "Who speaks for Wolf?" The tribal elders had forgotten to consider the natural inhabitants of the region—the wolves. This learning story illustrates the value of deep democracy and taking into consideration all participants in any decision.

I believe that this lesson provided the wisdom for my seeking inclusivity in the Forming the Future program. I often placed people with very disparate views on committees. For example, the analysis and research committee had both the editor of the *Austin American Statesman* and the leader of the Brown Berets involved in discussions. I attended many local school-community leadership meetings to scout emerging leadership in various school community and to invite those leaders to serve on the executive council. "Who speaks for wolf?" was the question I asked myself to determine if there were any marginalized participants or people left out of the Forming the Future process.

The spiritual influence of Ernest Holmes and Matthew Fox and of the Iroquois through the writings of Paula Spencer Underwood were instrumental in shaping my leadership of Forming the Future. From Ernest Holmes I learned about the law of attraction, mysticism, and how to direct the mind; from Matthew Fox I learned to put spirit into action in a way that creates justice, and from Paula Spencer Underwood I learned about how to think inclusively.

Chapter 6

Community Partnerships

In the civil rights movement, I discovered the power of community. As a student at North Texas State College in Denton, I was part of a community (facetiously called "The Clan") that participated in one of the early projects to integrate restaurants near campus and in northern Texas towns. My good friend and teacher Udah Mehta, a physics major from India who introduced me to the writings of Thomas Aquinas, the process philosophy of Alfred North Whitehead, and to the idea that God is energy, became a central figure in our movement, teaching the members of our group Gandhi's principles of nonviolence. As an enthusiastic student of government, I learned the case law related to civil rights in education.

Plessy v. Ferguson (Supreme Court, 1896) allowed separate but equal schools for blacks and whites. In the early fifties, racial segregation in public schools was the norm, and most black schools were inferior to white ones. In Topeka, Kansas, a black third grader named Linda Brown had to walk one mile through a railroad switchyard to get to her black elementary school, even though a white elementary school was only seven blocks away. Her father tried to enroll her in the white elementary school, but the principal of the school refused. Brown went to the Topeka branch of the NAACP and asked for help. Other black parents joined Brown in the complaint, which resulted in an injunction submitted by the NAACP that would forbid the segregation of Topeka schools. The district court agreed with the testimony that segregation was detrimental but because of *Plessy v. Ferguson* held in favor of the Board of Trustees. In 1954, in *Brown v. the Board of Education*, with Chief Justice Earl Warren writing the opinion,

the Supreme Court held that segregation deprives minority children of equal educational opportunities. This led to the desegregation of schools nationwide.

We felt that the segregation of the student union on the Denton campus was also not in keeping with equal opportunities in general. Applying the principles of nonviolent communication, these were the steps we took:

1. Negotiation of differences and an attempt to resolve them
2. Mobilization of supporters with proper nonviolent training
3. Demonstration of the issues, to seek support via petition, to try for resolution; but if this fails
4. Non-cooperation, including boycotts, strikes, peaceful disruption, blockades, and sit-ins; but if this fails
5. Creation of a Parallel Entity to replace the old opponent

The restaurant at the student union immediately made a change in its policy.

Almost 70 percent of the restaurants in Denton voluntarily desegregated after members of our group talked to them about the morality of desegregation. Our group was trained in nonviolent communication strategies at weekly meetings. For the remaining restaurants, we chose to picket and stage sit-ins. Sit-ins were done with whites and blacks. We sat at a table and waited to be served. Of course we never were served. Eventually, with the continued boycotting, picketing, and sit-ins, all the restaurants gave in and desegregated, if only for sheer economic reasons.

This effort in 1960 was the beginning of my social activism. Later I met and married my first husband, an exchange student from Bolivia who became the father of my two children. While he was completing graduate school in foreign languages, I took my first job in a Head Start program in 1967. It required teachers to visit the homes of their students, and it was my first experience with poverty. I visited all the homes of my students and attended the monthly advisory group meeting with the parents. Parents learned how to advocate for their children and get their needs met within the framework of public school hierarchies. It could be as simple as communicating with a teacher about a child's doctor's appointment or calling in when the child was sick.

Skills that I took for granted were foreign to impoverished parents. We empowered parents not to be afraid to communicate with teachers and principals.

To its credit, the Head Start program has included much more parental involvement than most state-funded or even private preschools. It required two home visits and two parent-teacher meetings yearly and supported parents in getting health insurance, medical care, social services, and adult education.

Parents also played a key role in governing local programs. Unfortunately, providing learning activities for parents to work with their children at home was not part of the early program design.

The next year I was asked to be the visiting teacher at the newly created bilingual school. The year after that I became both the principal of Creedmoor Bilingual School, in the Del Valle Independent School District, and the program director for the Title VII grant. In the Title VII Bilingual Program, I worked with a parent advisory committee that had oversight of our grant and a parent-involvement program. We were staffed with a parent-involvement coordinator who was charged with educating parents and keeping the lines of communication open between school and home. One of my early actions was to create a monthly clinic that met at the school and brought in social service agencies from Austin so that parents in our rural community could have better access to resources that existed some thirty miles away in that city.

I learned firsthand that while the PTA attracted women, the business of looking at grant budgets and setting educational goals attracted men to become involved at the Creedmoor Bilingual School. The involvement of men extended to facilities needs, as one man donated air conditioners to our school when no other school in the district had air-conditioning. "How did you get those air conditioners?" I was asked by other teachers in the district. "Through parent involvement," I always replied. "Get your parents involved." I loved working with the parents and instilling in them a love of education. I believe education is the way to freedom and greater economic mobility for children. One Hispanic mom said that she told her son, "When you get to eighth grade, I can't help you with your homework anymore. That's when I quit school. But you will study, I'll make sure of that!"

Not only were minority parents involved, but also I hired some of them to be teacher's aides. This boosted the economic level of the community. This school received numerous awards for academic excellence within a tristate area. Five years later, I was recruited by the former Del Valle superintendent to the educational development department of the Austin Independent School District to head its new Model Cities Program.

The Model Cities Program, which I directed from 1972 to '75, provided for dynamic parent-involvement training so that parents could learn how to advocate more effectively for their children's success in school and teach their children at home. The program had a million-dollar budget, which was funded through three sources: Title I, Model Cities, and the City of Austin. It supported four experimental schools in a communication-skills project in four extremely impoverished areas in East Austin. It had a large parental-involvement component, with a parent advisory group that met monthly and quarterly trainings of an educational nature.

In addition to designing the reading- and oral-language components of the school program, I developed a home intervention program called Happy Talk, based upon Phyllis Levenstein's research on early childhood intervention. It was predicated on the idea that parents can be trained to interact verbally with their children (age two to five) and thus enhance the possibility of their children's success in first grade. My own research showed similar promise. It was therefore shocking to learn that early childhood funding was decreased instead of increased when it was shown that gaps between poor and rich children could be reduced through educational intervention.

In Kansas City, Betty Hart and Todd Risley, while developing an early childhood program, discovered that there were distinct differences in language development related to family income. By recording every word spoken by children and parents, these researchers found that average four-year-olds in families whose parents are professionals are exposed to thirty-two million more words than four-year-olds whose parents receive public assistance (Hart and Risley 2003).

Even more important, affluent parents showered their children with encouragement while welfare parents—reflecting the greater stress in their lives—offered less praise and more frequent criticism. By third grade, the children's success in school mirrored their vocabulary growth at age three, which closely tracked the levels of positive stimulation by their parents. In fact, differences in parenting during the first three years were far more powerful predictors of success in third grade than socioeconomic status.

Hart and Risley were not the first to suggest that parents play a crucial role in their children's success, of course. But their eye-opening data raises an important question: How can we hope to "leave no child behind" if we do not first help disadvantaged parents give their children richer and more positive support in the early years?

Consider the success of efforts like Phyllis Levenstein's Parent-Child Home Program, a program I personally visited in the early 1970s in New York City. The program had begun in the mid-1960s, with Levenstein training home visitors to go into the homes of new parents and teach them positive parenting strategies, using books and toys that were gifted to the participating families. Twice weekly, for the better part of two years, these visitors went to the homes of two- and three-year-olds, bringing gifts for the child and sitting with the parent and child while modeling positive parenting behaviors.

The strategy worked, and it continued to work with more than four thousand children each year at 139 sites nationwide. In South Carolina, a 2002 study found that a mostly African American group of first graders who had participated in the program as tots scored far above the average of other poor children for school readiness and even above district and state averages. A long-term follow-up in Pittsfield, Massachusetts, found that at-risk children who took part in the program had a high school–graduation rate of 84 percent, compared with 53 percent for eligible children who did not participate. Today a mountain of evidence suggests that by combining parental support with high-quality childcare, the school-readiness gap can practically be eliminated for poor children.

Happy Talk also employed people from the community as home demonstrators, and the program obtained positive results, suggesting that this type of intervention with parents can have a positive effect on lessening the academic gap between advantaged children and their impoverished counterparts (Bingham 1974).

Community involvement is a very powerful thing. My home was destroyed in the 1981 Austin, Texas, Memorial Day flood. In the aftermath, a neighbor invited me to her house for an informal discussion about the flood. At the meeting I found myself volunteering to organize a neighborhood association that would give us more leverage in the city. I wrote up a petition to establish the Johnson Creek Neighborhood Restoration Association with a one-dollar membership fee to join. I walked to all the houses along the creek within a two-mile radius and signed up about thirty enthusiastic members. My neighbor made her house available for the meetings.

A local politician attended and presented the idea of additional street drains being installed to address the flood. Our neighborhood could get the drains moved up on the planning improvements schedule for the city simply by lobbying at a council meeting for the change. All we had to do was make an appearance at the city council chambers. Later that week, we held another meeting with the city engineer. He was talking about drains too. Finally, I asked, "Will that solve the problem?" He hesitated and was honest enough to say that it would not. The only thing that would permanently solve the flooding problem in the Johnson Creek neighborhood would be a bypass. "How much does that cost?" I asked. "Five million," he answered.

In my research on the neighborhood, I learned that the Mopac Highway was built so that its runoff water intentionally drained into Johnson Creek. There was liability both from the federal government and the city for past decisions made: laws were in place that prohibited water from being drained into neighborhood waterways.

The following week, we stood outside the city council meeting in the lobby gathered as a neighborhood organization. The politician came in and said, "Why aren't you sitting inside?" I gathered the neighbors around me to caucus and said, "I think we should go for the permanent solution—the bypass." En masse, we walked out of city hall. The next few months we organized meetings with planning commission members and city council members. We secured commitments for a bypass.

I was not present when the champagne bottle was cracked over Johnson Creek some eight years later, because by that time I was living in Seattle attending ministerial school, but the injustice had been corrected and the neighborhood would most likely never flood again.

My experiences in community taught me that great things are possible when parents and community are unified around big goals. It was only natural for me to be comfortable about inviting the citizens of Austin to join in Forming the Future.

Chapter 7

Crisis and Opportunity

"No one on the cabinet believes a bond issue can be passed," said a friend to me confidentially. It was the kind of pronouncement I loved to defy. I thought of the Chinese symbol for crisis that also means opportunity.

The Austin Independent School District was a large urban school district that encompassed 230 square miles, with 55,300 students, of whom 15,900 were in high school, some 8,700 in junior high, and 29,800 in elementary school. It had 7,000 special education students, with 2,600 served in integrated or self-contained programs. The racial ethnic percentages of the student body were 19 percent African American, 28 percent Hispanic, and 53 percent white, distributed consistently from kindergarten through twelfth grade.

In 1981, the Austin school district faced a huge crisis: it was unable to provide enough classrooms for its student bodies. More than five thousand students were assigned to 201 portable buildings. Demographic projections showed that over 14,000 additional children would be attending the Austin schools by 1990. Nine new elementary schools, three junior high schools, and one high school were recommended, as well as major additions to existing schools. All these repairs and new schools would have to be funded by a bond issue presented to the public for a vote. Who would turn out to vote?

For the last ten years, Austin had been in litigation over its desegregation plan. In one plan, it had classified Mexican American children as white, causing all the Hispanic organizations to protest. In December of 1979, a consent decree was signed by all parties, ending 9 ½ years of litigation. Some fifteen thousand students were to be bussed. On December 10, 1979, three hundred Anderson High School students stormed the administration building chanting "Hell, no, we won't go." The desegregation issue had caused several citizen committees, who had assembled to organize bond issues, to declare there was too much enmity and passing bonds would be impossible. The district had gone for thirteen years without a bond issue. If systems, like individuals, can experience emptying and loss, then the Austin Independent School District was in its dark night of the soul, or Via Negativa. In the citizenry and staff, there was a sense of despair about the future.

To cap it off, there was an economic downturn. In 1982, Texas went from a budget surplus of $2.5 billion to a projected deficit of about $3 billion in 1987. In 1980, it had one of the lowest unemployment rates (5.3 percent), and by mid-

1986 that had risen to the highest unemployment rate ever (about 11 percent). The oil economy was the factor. A decrease of one dollar in the cost per barrel of crude oil impacts the jobs of 25,000 Texans. At the time, Austin's economy had not diversified into high-technology business as it has today. A high percentage of school-bond issues were failing nationwide at this time.

Shortly after the arrival of John Ellis, the new superintendent of schools, my friend David, who was assistant superintendent, ran into me in the cafeteria of the Austin Independent School District. "Well, how is the new superintendent?" I asked. I hadn't met him yet. David replied almost cryptically, "The superintendent is looking for an idea to unify the community."

I immediately knew why he was telling me this. It was a call. I was in the creative department of the district, developmental programs. It was my job to come up with ideas. I did not know at the time how these words would form my future: "He's been told that the community isn't interested in participation." Well, I knew that wasn't the truth.

The wheels in my mind began to turn. I had always been a history buff because it gives me a sense of the morphic field of a city and suggests an

action to be taken in the present. I was scanning a scrapbook of Austin's history and discovered a story about how the school system began one hundred years previously. The first superintendent of schools had invited children, parents, and teachers to a picnic in Pease Park. In my imagination I could see this event being reenacted.

There was one problem, however. Pease Park couldn't hold the numbers of people I was anticipating would participate. I had studied research about school improvement programs that used an appreciative inquiry process of discovering what was good, what needed improvement and an ideal future. I outlined a project design that would involve the twenty-two newly desegregated element schools, using an assessment tool that would allow participants to do just that.

I submitted it to the new superintendent. He responded within a week, giving me permission to organize it. The kickoff day was the first Saturday in May. I sent each school instructions on how to form school-community leadership teams, inviting them to the May meeting. I designed training materials for them to take back to their community to gather information and conduct surveys.

To my amazement five hundred people showed up on that sunny Saturday morning.

Most of the schools had teams of principals, parents, and teachers. The superintendent was impressed and, spinning toward me, said, "Where's the press?" I hadn't thought about publicizing the event. When the workshop was concluded, the participants were infused with high enthusiasm. It showed the superintendent that community building was possible in Austin, even in a time of mild economic depression, desegregation, and a thirteen-year absence of any large-scale community involvement in the public schools. This moment was the seed of what was to come. All the schools turned in reports, based on community surveys, which I summarized for the superintendent. I had accomplished what I set out to do: to prove that the Austin community was still interested in its schools.

The new superintendent had a good track record in organizing the community. He had a goal of unifying the community to pass a bond issue. Dr. John Ellis came from Columbus, Ohio, where during his tenure a snowstorm had incapacitated the schools, and he had succeeded in rallying the community, schools, and media to put the entire school curriculum on local television stations so that the children could continue their lessons at home. He had witnessed solid community support in action and had been hired to unify the district and pass a bond issue.

Nothing happened. The hot summer moved on. My neighborhood was engaged in cleanup after the one-hundred-year flood. Our creek bed was cleaned out by the city. We organized to feed the workers fried chicken with iced soft drinks. In the meantime, my husband and I moved out of the house because of the mold. We rented an apartment. My own personal life continued to be in crisis. We felt that living in our flooded house was not viable. Yet renting an apartment and paying a mortgage represented a financial challenge. I asked my ex-husband if he would take my two children to California to live. Then August rolled around and everything began to change. Forming the Future would become the lovely dream cocoon that would provide my home away from home.

Part II
The Project Itself

Chapter 8

Chosen to Form the Future

Our deepest fear is not that we are inadequate. Our deepest fear is that we are powerful beyond measure. It is our light, not our darkness that most frightens us. We ask ourselves, Who am I to be brilliant, gorgeous, talented, fabulous? Actually, who are you *not* to be? You are a child of God. Your playing small does not serve the world. There is nothing enlightened about shrinking so that other people won't feel insecure around you. We are all meant to shine, as children do. We were born to make manifest the glory of God that is within us. It's not just in some of us; it's in everyone. And as we let our own light shine, we unconsciously give other people permission to do the same. As we are liberated from our own fear, our presence automatically liberates others.
—Marianne Williamson, *A Return to Love*

After my experiment with twenty-two schools, very little happened for a few months. Then in early August the superintendent called and asked me to meet with him. My friend in the evaluation department, Freda Holley, had told me the week before that she had come up with a name for the superintendent's project: Forming the Future. Dr. Holley had the laser-sharp mind of a Vance Packard and could envision scenarios that played out in the future. I was not surprised that she came up with such a fabulous name for a project. But the project had little else other than a name. The superintendent had seen the pilot project I did with twenty-two schools and saw my ease in working with the community.

At the meeting, the superintendent said, "I want you to direct Forming the Future. I have two main goals for the project: unify the community and pass a bond issue."

I was very excited about the prospect of this new position and accepted immediately. He said, "Give me your budget tomorrow morning and go down to personnel and see what kind of salary you will qualify for in this new position. I think there's an empty office in the basement right below my office." He informed my boss of my impending transfer.

It was clear that in accepting the position I was one of the few people besides the superintendent who truly believed that accomplishing the goals of Forming the Future was possible. I was not the first pick. Or even the second. But I was picked because I embodied a belief that it could be done. The person who can with confidence look into the future and still remain in the now moment and not look backward will demonstrate a supremacy of spiritual thought over any material resistance. That was what I discovered to be the secret of Forming the Future.

The superintendent's faith in me was a major contribution to my success. He gave me free rein and his total confidence. He told me I had a month to develop the program design and training that was to be presented at the first principals' meeting in mid-September. It was early August 1981. I knew I could do it. I had a deep faith in the community built from my experience in parent involvement from Head Start to bilingual programs to Model Cities. I had previously designed a training program on effective practices for desegregated schools and wrote the training modules so that the principals could train their own faculties without outside consultants. Now I was being challenged to create a program that would unify the whole community. I had just been granted a chance to not play small. I knew Forming the Future was a really big thing. A lot was riding on it.

Faith operating through humans has built mental attitudes, businesses, educational institutions, wars, and even efforts for peace. Faith shapes the universe of the future. It exists where our attention is focused and always works to bring into manifestation what we truly believe. Faith can be used negatively or positively. Too many leaders did not believe a bond issue was possible in the climate that existed in 1981. I believed in the value of the public schools. I believed all children were entitled to a good education and to good facilities in which to learn. I believed that the Austin community, over half of which was college educated, held a value of an educated citizenry and would support its public schools with a bond issue.

At the same time I was chosen to form the district's future, I realized at some deep level I would be postponing forming my own personal life. My second marriage was very conflicted. The Memorial Day flood had destroyed my home. My two children, aged eleven and sixteen, moved to California to live with their father. My husband and I abandoned living in our house and moved into an apartment. He had been disabled by an automobile accident a year earlier, wore a leg brace, and reluctantly explored ways to rebuild the house on its existing lot.

For two years, I lived in the dream of Forming the Future, which was more rewarding than focusing on all the personal dilemmas at home. I ignored any evidence that my personal future was not moving forward: there were no house plans, and my husband was so depressed and volatile I didn't dare ask about anything. Forming the Future became my refuge from the storm. The constant abrasive quality of my home life became the irritation that produced the pearl—a program design that succeeded beyond all expectations.

In Buddhism, one takes refuge in what is known as the "three jewels," which are Buddha, Dharma, and the Sangha. The Buddha is the human who attains enlightenment while sitting under a bodhi tree in India. Dharma refers to the teachings of the Buddha, and the sangha is the community of people who take refuge in the Buddha and the Dharma. It is really about taking refuge in someone who has let go of holding back.

In this context, my first jewel was the superintendent who held the highest vision for my achievement with the project. My second refuge was in his teachings, his encouragement to let go of holding back, and his invitation to create the impossible dream. My third jewel was found among the community of people in Austin who shared a longing to not hold back the good from their schools. You could say the project became both my religion and my home. As Karen Armstrong writes, "Human beings cannot endure emptiness and desolation; they will fill the vacuum by creating a new focus of meaning" (1993, 199). My new focus of meaning allowed me to fully accept present moments as they unfolded and to give up struggling in exchange for something more powerful: the reception of the community's will for good.

In *Leading Minds: An Anatomy of Leadership*, Howard Gardner and Emma Laskin (1995) find six constants of leadership:

1. The Story – "A leader must have a central story or message." Gandhi had a message of including Muslims in his vision of India. Gardner notes that there are always exclusionary and inclusionary forces vying with each other. For example, the identity story of Martin Luther King Jr. was, "We blacks must stand up for our rights and do so non-violently" (Ibid., 308) and of Eleanor Roosevelt, "We women can and should be full of participants in the political life of the nation, and we should stand up for what we believe is right" (Ibid., 309). My story was "We can save our public schools and benefit all children."

2. The Audience – Leaders can effect small change in an already knowledgeable group and are challenged to bring about change in a large, heterogeneous group. I was able to effect a small change in the educators, and then, through involvement of community, to bring about a change in a larger more inclusive group.

3. The Organization – Enduring leadership requires an organization. It is the leader's job to bring the organization along. Ernest Holmes agreed to establish an organization so that his writings and philosophy could be perpetuated. Margaret Mead (1901–1978), an American cultural anthropologist who earned her PhD from Columbia University and became a communicator of anthropology through her books. Margaret Mead spurned organizational commitments, and as a result there is no school of "Mead" after her death.

Forming the Future could not have been possible without the existing institution of a school district with its extensive networks and systems. I was able to bring the organization along with the project.

4. The Embodiment – Leaders must embody their stories, even though they do not have to be saints. I truly believed in the process and in the positive change the program was accomplishing.

5. Direct and Indirect Leadership – Gardner and Laskin remark that Margaret Mead and Robert Oppenheimer provided direct leadership within their domains. Vaclav Havel of the Czech Republic provided political leadership. Direct leadership is more tumultuous and risky. Indirect leaders have time for reflection and revision. Sometimes a leader can achieve a political end by working through existing political leadership rather than taking power directly on a personal platform. My work in Forming the Future was an example of indirect leadership, where I worked through existing political and civic organizations rather than from a personal platform. The superintendent and board of trustees were the direct political leaders.

6. Expertise – A leader is unlikely to achieve credibility unless her work is of high quality. The more involved individuals become in direct leadership, the less time they have to retain their technical expertise. Gardner and Laskin note the paradox that "direct leaders typically lack direct knowledge, while indirect leaders often can proceed on the basis of direct knowledge. How to attain and maintain expertise is an acute problem for anyone who aspires to direct leadership, and particularly for those who wish to direct a heterogeneous group on the basis of the best current information drawn from the most relevant domains" (Ibid., 290–295).

Forming the Future involved taking expert knowledge, judging its importance, and then communicating it to the general public. On the one hand, the best information is wanted upon which to base decisions after it has been digested and weighed. On the other hand, most leaders and their audiences do not have time to master the information or issues. Daniel Bell says, "The person who can strike the right balance between the sense of complexity and the sense of judgment is increasingly rare, and that is a problem it seems to me in every society" (Ibid., 301).

My leadership in Forming the Future was enhanced by having an authoritative position as special assistant to the superintendent as well as by my own agency and powers of persuasion. I have come to appreciate that a few individuals matter a great deal and that those who choose to put forth an inclusionary story can make a difference.

Chapter 9

Sitting for an Idea

Mothering is allowing things to develop in your mind
according to their own timing.
—Rev. Deborah L. Johnson, *The Sacred Yes*

After I was promoted, I remember going to my new office in the basement of the school administration building. I had gotten approval for my $100,000 budget for the year. I sat down all alone in a quiet room, contemplating how to engage public participation and support. At first, I remember spending hours in a state of emptiness and silence. This lasted for almost a month.

The word *concentrate* means "to bring to a point." To concentrate the mentality means to bring one's thinking to bear on one point of interest and hold it there. Concentration has little to do with willpower. My discovery was that in focused meditation about how to organize this program, messages and ideas began to come to me in dreams—including a programmatic design—and in flashes. The program seemed to naturally unfold.

I found that by concentrating on some particular idea or thought, it was important to keep my attention on it—but without effort. At first, my attention wavered, but I learned to make no mental effort and just feel at ease, gently bringing my attention back to the idea. It is usually a mistake to oppose thoughts that interfere, because in resisting something the whole reflection is disrupted. Concentration is always from within and never from without. The only place that the mind can know is within itself.

In concentrating, I laid aside all willpower and resistance, and just allowed the mind to give me the most prolific of results. The first thing to emerge was a picture. It was an arrow that contained the phases of the program: grassroots school-community leadership teams, coordinating council, executive committee.

What emerged from hours of contemplation, intense concentration, and research was Forming the Future, a model focused on high-quality study by citizens as well as deep listening and discussion by school-community leadership teams. It also involved district-level focus groups, which addressed specific organizational questions and involved a majority of citizens. Each committee included a few staff resource people to address specific organizational questions. The design of these focus groups was flexible and their topics a response to community interest.

Five goals came into view during the program's genesis:

1. Create a long-range plan supported by the community for the future of Austin Independent School District.
2. Develop citizen support for facility improvement leading to a successful bond election.
3. Provide for curriculum renewal.
4. Develop a financial plan ensuring high-quality education at a reasonable cost.
5. Increase citizen participation in the programs of Austin Independent School District.

I believed strongly in the public schools as an avenue of justice for the poor and rich. The naysayers claimed our schools were headed downhill due to desegregation and other trends, such as people moving to the suburbs. My intention was to create an inclusive way of recommitting the public to its schools.

How was I able to lead such a project? I believe I was uniquely qualified to lead this project. Not only did I have the faith, but also I had a unique background in Creation Spirituality principles, the spiritual teachings of

Gandhi, and the Iroquois vision of spiritual democracy that influenced the design of this project and guided my leadership. I put this into book form because over the course of two decades I have not seen this program replicated and everyone to whom I have talked about this project has said "You ought to write a book about that."

Forming the Future had its roots in the invisible energy of the nonmaterial world that is always available, always in reach of those who give direction to their faith. Forming the Future became a living reality. I had no idea how anything would be formed. I truly had a beginner's mind. I followed my intuition.

I drafted a letter for the superintendent to send to all corporations in Austin, inviting them to participate in the project. We asked the editorial board of the newspaper to endorse it. They agreed to publicize this opportunity for involvement. The phone rang constantly with calls from hundreds of people interested in participating; many sent in resumes and asked how they could contribute. Some dressed up and dropped by my office and begged to be involved as if they were applying for the job of a lifetime. I involved everyone who contacted me, telling them that the district-level part of the project would begin in January. I developed a tentative outline of committees for the project, which kept expanding as people indicated new interests.

The survey I developed used elements of *appreciative inquiry*, although at the time I was unaware of the term. The survey was not fixed but flexible; it was organic and responsive to community feedback.

Flexible and Open at the Top

The district-level portion of the program began with a skeletal list of committees I thought would be important. The superintendent of schools met with the editorial board of the newspaper and secured the paper's endorsement of the project. The newspaper printed an interview with me, requesting volunteers to participate on citizen committees to "form the future" of the schools. The response of the citizenry to the article was overwhelming. When I would tell them about the committee options, often another concern would surface, and I was able to form a new committee, ending up with thirty-four of them. I felt it was very important for me to be "open at the top" to new information as it emerged.

Thus, the organizational structure sprang from the interests and needs of the citizenry. Sets of questions were written for each committee to explore. We scheduled a meeting of all volunteers in February 1982. The group also included interested individuals from local schools. Over four hundred citizens showed up for the initial orientation and then met in committees to plan a course of action and subsequent meetings to explore their particular charge.

Prior to my accepting the position as assistant to the superintendent for Forming the Future, I had designed an in-service program using the latest educational research on desegregated schools in thirteen separate modules, organized and scripted for the principals to deliver to their faculty, complete with handouts. The project was created in response to the need for retraining in newly desegregated schools and out of necessity, since there were no funds to hire outside consultants to do staff training. I conducted a training session for the principals, who in turn conducted two days of training in their own schools. It was very successful. I was familiar with the National Diffusion Network, which published *Educational Programs That Work* (online, n.d.), providing examples of programs that defined their implementation requirements. I had been trained in temporary project management because throughout my career in education most of my work was done on temporary projects with soft money. Forming the Future would not be an exception. It was a two-year temporary project, after which I would go back into another department.

I had also worked in the developmental programs department of the district on several projects with the University of Texas Research and Development Center. I was particularly familiar with Gene E. Hall and Shirley M. Hord's work *Change in Schools: Facilitating the Process*. From their standpoint, there are several important assumptions about change:

1. Understanding the point of view of the participants in the change process is critical.
2. Change is a process, not an event.

3. It is possible to anticipate much that will occur during a change process.
4. Innovations come in all sizes and shapes.
5. Innovation and implementation are two sides of the change-process coin.
6. To change something, someone has to change first.
7. Everyone can be a change facilitator.

(Hall and Hord 1987, 8–11)

In this model, as the project director, I would have the job of facilitating or assisting others in ways relevant to their concerns so they could become more effective and skilled in using new programs and procedures.

What was the innovation of Forming the Future? What were its key features? If implemented successfully, Forming the Future promised a *relative advantage* to the school district as a whole and to schools individually. It could build and repair schools. It could also get community support for needed curriculum reform. For the board and superintendent, success would be measured by the passage of a bond issue, and with the money to implement necessary repairs, more money could be allocated to curriculum and program development.

Then there was the aspect of complexity of the project. The twenty-two pilot schools were required to organize a school-community leadership team, talk about things they liked and things that needed improvement, survey their community, and make recommendations for improving their school. In the Forming the Future project, the innovations did not appear to be complex. There were four parts:

1. School-Community Leadership Teams in eighty-one schools meet in the fall and make suggestions for improvement of their schools, recommending items to be included in bond issue for facilities improvements; staff prepares a summary document of recommendations.
2. Coordinating Council makes suggestions for improvement of district programs; staff prepares a summary document of recommendations.

3. Executive Committee, with representation from all levels, synthesizes all information and prioritizes all recommendations into a report to the board of trustees.

4. A bond issue is passed; change recommendations are implemented.

Feasibility was a major factor in the implementation. Since twenty-two schools had already successfully tried a component of Forming the Future, it seemed less risky to try it with eighty-one schools. The superintendent had seen the excitement of five hundred people, and he had seen me train them the previous spring before Forming the Future began.

Goals needed to be clear and well defined for both the schools and the public at large. I established the five goals for the project. The superintendent had charged me with goals 2 and 5 from the project's inception, but as I did my early intuitive research and talked to people in the community, I discovered that the community felt additional goals (1, 3, and 4) were important to gain full community support and the endorsement of a bond issue. It is not sufficient to have just a goals-and-outcomes orientation. Administrators, teachers, and others may not know exactly what they need to do to achieve the outcomes that were obtained in the earlier pilot project.

Defining the Requirements for Forming the Future

After I was assigned the formidable task to create Forming the Future, the superintendent said that the implementation requirements needed to be ready for the general principals' meeting in mid-September. I reviewed many resources that modeled effective community organizing strategies, which I adapted for use by the school-community leadership teams. The manual I developed for the principals, which is included in the appendix of this book, included the following sections:

Organizing the School-Community Leadership Team
Reaching Out to the Community to Build the Team
Gathering Information
Surveying the Community

Looking at the Building and Curriculum Needs
Making Recommendations

The components for implementation of the first phase of the Forming the Future program at the grassroots level included the following:

Training Manual for Principals
Survey of Parents/Community
Techniques for Organizing School-Community Leadership Team
Timeline for Completion

We anticipated the possibility that principals might not feel comfortable with handling conflict if it were to occur in the school-community leadership team meetings. We therefore provided some training by an outside consultant on conflict resolution and how to "think on your feet." What I had not anticipated was that the principals had very little experience in conducting community advisory meetings. I had been schooled in all kinds of parent-involvement programs from Head Start to Title I and Title VII programs, all of which had parent advisory groups. Most of the principals, however, had only experienced PTA organizations, a very different kind of structure. What was needed was a script with how to organize and conduct a community meeting for the purpose of Forming the Future.

The first resistance to the innovation came at a principals' meeting the week after the principals received their manuals. There was rumbling. I was startled by the negativity so soon in the process. The assistant superintendent of elementary education deftly coaxed out their concerns as I stood and listened. Anytime the principals needed more information, I responded. Some evenings I was invited to speak before groups of parents at schools. Other evenings I went out and visited meetings of the teams at several individual schools. Each day different things happened, and I was able to respond, moment to moment.

While Phase I at the grass roots was going on, I initiated Phase II. This involved getting a newspaper article in the *Austin Statesman* about the project and soliciting volunteers both for the grassroots phase and the coordinating-council phase. An earlier meeting of the superintendent, school board president, and editorial board had secured an endorsement of the project by the newspaper. I also developed an informational piece to use as an overview of the project to interested community members and people in the school district.

Most of the people who advised me had thought the coordinating council would be the typical bond-campaign committee of one hundred citizens. That would be a simple innovation, right? Forming the Future seemed to have a life of its own. Because after the newspaper article calling for volunteers I had received all those hundreds of reactions, I initially created six main areas of focus for the district-level process: Education (Curriculum), Facilities, Finance, Personnel, Analysis, and Community Relations.

Underneath each broad area was a sketch of possible subcommittees. I had anticipated five hundred people participating at this level, but instead we had 3,500. Every conversation with a potential volunteer became an incident intervention, but it was a very fluid process. If a committee did not exist to discuss the gifted and talented, and a person wanted to address this issue, I created the subcommittee. That is how we ended up with thirty-four different subcommittees. The February meeting was set to follow the completion of the school-community leadership team grassroots phase.

At the same time, I needed to recruit a community chair to head up the Forming the Future program on the citizen side of the equation. I came into this job skilled in innovation, educational research, staff and program development, but with absolutely no knowledge of the Austin community. I had never worked in any community-relations position prior to this job other than the parent advisory committees, which involved very specific populations and were geared to a specific target audience. How would I find the perfect person who could bring together the whole community?

As I reflected on this, with a beginner's mind, I got the idea of going to the school district archival files in the superintendent's office. I remember sitting on the floor in front of an old file cabinet in a little nook. There I found lists of community members who had served on various advisory committees, curriculum committees, bond issue campaigns, and those who even had served on school boards. It was a treasure trove of names of people whom I had never met. There was one name that surfaced over and over again within a twenty-year time frame: Willie Kocurek.

Mr. Kocurek had been president of the school board and had actively supported the schools over a long period of time. In asking around, I learned he was the oldest person to ever graduate from the University of Texas Law School. I wasted no time in setting up an appointment with him. I explained all about Forming the Future and its importance and why I thought he was the one to chair it. He was flabbergasted and told me I had the wrong person. He could see it was a major undertaking. I should be talking to his son, Neal, who was president of Radian Corporation.

"No," I said, listening to my intuition. "*You* are the one I want." He said he would have to talk it over with his wife. I told him that if he was interested, the superintendent would want to talk to him too.

The next day, Willie Kocurek called me back with the thrilling news that he would accept the challenge of Forming the Future. I set up a meeting between Willie and the superintendent, who was equally delighted by the choice.

My perfect ally had arrived. Willie Kocurek was the community-relations director of a local bank and was very plugged into the community through years of community service in the Downtown Lions Club, the University Methodist Church, the Gray Panthers, and numerous other networks. He readily recruited his cadre of stable leaders into the Forming the Future process, and together we reviewed the hundreds of resumes of others, met with each individual, and appointed the chairs of each committee. By February, we were ready for the community meeting of the coordinating council.

My beginner's mind had been a powerful attractor of a great community leader who was friend to the multitudes. Not only did he seem to know about everybody, but also he had a charismatic way of getting them involved. Within fifteen minutes, he could call thirty Lions Club members and invite them to his law office for pizza and persuade them to all join in his next project. I fell in love with this seventy-year-old dynamo. His name for me was "Miss Wow." The next year and a half we worked together as a team. It turned out to be a partnership made in heaven.

Willie Kocurek was born in 1910 in a small farmhouse in the tiny central Texas community of Dimebox, the son of Czechoslovakian immigrants. His parents were interested in education and had their children study their lessons around a long wooden table. Later, the family moved several times to Marlin, Durango, and then to Caldwell, where Willie attended high school and found his "somebody" as he called her, his mentor and coach, Leigh Peck, who taught him debate and English. She decided he should go to the University of Texas at Austin and drove him there in her automobile. She arranged for him to get a job at the Grayburg Oil Company, which assigned him to pump gas at a station not far from the university. He graduated with honors with a bachelor's in business administration in 1933.

He continued to work in the filling station business and by that time had married Maurine, the love of his life. He bought a bigger filling station and joined the Lion's Club. Then his life in Austin was interrupted by a stint in the Navy. When it ended in 1946, he returned home and got back into the filling station business. He later opened an appliance business, making it easy for people to establish credit.

Willie always wore his trademark red bow tie. His slogans, such as "You don't need money, just a little bit a month" and "Where there's a Willie, there's a way," had endeared him to masses of people who were given flexible ways to pay for their appliances. In 1946, he ran for the Austin School Board and was elected. In 1950, he became president of the board. That was the year the district held its first bond campaign for $7.5 million. After eight years on the board, he went back to working full-time in his business.

By the time he and Maurine reached their sixties, there was still a dream Willie had not yet realized. When he had first come to Austin in 1929, he had dreamed of going to law school. Fifty years later, he entered the University of Texas Law School, and, at the age of seventy, he acquired the distinction of being the oldest person to ever graduate from law school. He started his own law firm with two other lawyers. He was approached by Westlake Bank with an offer to work for them in community relations, which he accepted. That was the job he held when I invited him to chair Forming the Future. In perfect tribute to this tireless community leader, one of the newly built elementary schools was named Willie I. Kocurek Elementary School, which was completed in 1986. Charismatic and kind, wise and witty, Willie had been the perfect choice to form the future of the Austin schools.

Leadership Tools

While directing Forming the Future, I discovered that everyone involved needed a training manual that told them exactly how to involve their school community. Sometimes the information provided in the manual was insufficient for those involved. It was important that I listened to the need for additional details and information from principals who were charged with leading the school-community-leadership-team process. Toward that end, the two assistant superintendents in charge of secondary and elementary education helped facilitate that communication, albeit sometimes with pleas for help.

Listening to these communications and meeting the principals' need for details was extremely important. One of the early issues that emerged was that many did not know how to conduct a community meeting. I wrote them a script for the event. Some of them felt uncomfortable in handling conflict. I contracted with some highly skilled trainers to work with the principals on communication skills and conflict resolution. Amazingly, those principals who followed the directions in the manual secured very dynamic community participation. The manual directed principals to go beyond parents and involve local businesses and community leaders in their school-community leadership teams. The principals were told to seek out broad participation because less than one-third of the voters had children in school.

Over the course of two years, I handled personality clashes, detailed the intention of the project, prevented efforts to cut the bond issue in half, handled personnel issues, power plays, public hearings, time constraints, and rapid change on a day-to-day basis. It took a while to put in place an effective staff. One temporary employee treated the project like a slow-paced volunteer undertaking. Another potential employee revealed an ego-driven persona, and I backed away from hiring him. In the end, my secretary and assistant, Lois Hart, worked to bring the project to closure along with the very able assistance of an executive committee of twenty people.

Working with the chairman, Willie Kocurek, was like working with my alter ego. He was uplifting and exemplary as a leader. Without his enthusiastic support the project would never have been accomplished.

His networks in the community tapped into known leadership and created the pool of leadership needed for the thirty-four subcommittees. They say leaders fall into three categories: responders *let* it happen; managers *help* it happen; initiators *make* it happen. Willie Kocurek was an *initiator*. He was the wind beneath my sails.

Forming the Future was a community-involvement process that modeled spiritual democracy. It offered a way to transform and reinvent education. The meaning of the word *education* comes from the Latin *educare*, meaning to draw out of. The program I designed drew out the wisdom of over twenty thousand people.

Chapter 10

Listening to Dissent

It was well past eight o'clock when I walked into the Austin Independent School District administration building. It was late summer of 1982 and nearly dark. I sat down in my work area behind a screen in the back of my office and began to reflect upon the next steps of Forming the Future.

A year had passed so fast, and already the twenty-member executive committee was appointed. We refined massive amounts of information from eighty-one school communities and thirty-four subcommittees and had compiled them into a cogent set of recommendations in a final report to the board of trustees. This committee worked tirelessly over the entire summer to identify and agree upon certain broad criteria for determining priorities and to review the recommendations from the facilities committee for the bond issue. It was in the middle of this process, in the heat of summer, when it seemed all the hard work was going to be undermined.

My reflections were disrupted by noise coming from the hall: the voices of the man who had wanted to have my job and whose office was next door and of his buddy, an engineer from IBM who served as a member of the Forming the Future facilities committee. They were reviewing details of a facilities plan. The engineer was discussing a computer model for desegregation he had applied to the projections for future schools. In his estimation, three schools were not needed. I thought nothing of it—until

I heard my name mentioned. "How do you suppose we can get this past Frances?" "I don't know. She's pretty solid with the executive committee."

I sat in silence, stunned. Did they know I was in the next room? I concluded they did not because they continued to plot and scheme about how they could get political acceptance of a plan that would reduce the number of schools to be built based on an assumption of "white flight," which they theorized would greatly alter the demographic projections justifying the construction of new schools. Throughout their conversation, I didn't move. I barely breathed.

They left abruptly, turning out the light and exiting through the door at the end of the hallway. Virtually paralyzed, I stayed for another half hour. The thought of conflict was unnerving. I had grown up in a household where conflict rarely occurred, and when it did, an argument was usually shut down by my mother to maintain the peace. Now I was leading a process that involved thousands of people in discussions about the future of their public schools. Surely, with all those people coming together, there would be conflict. I had to be kidding myself that it would be sunshine and roses.

What course of action would I pursue? My first reaction was to want to retaliate. I wanted to shut my "opponents" down. This so-called plan of theirs had not emerged from the group consensus but through their backroom machinations: two people plotting secretly, determined to get their point of view adopted. Initially, I was upset and angry that a colleague would do this. I had not left him out of the process. I had invited him to serve as a staff resource to the committee on desegregation, his area of expertise. This was certainly another voice, or what Arnold Mindell would label a "Time Spirit," that wanted to be heard. For example, I held the optimistic belief that the issue of school desegregation would not affect public school support by the community. However, some parents were disenchanted with the system after desegregation. These voices in the night represented a "Time Spirit" for a hidden concern that was not vocalized elsewhere. Who would want to publicly admit to not liking a system in which their children were on a bus up to two hours a day? If a voice is not articulated, Mindell says, it modulates into a ghost or "Time Spirit" that, if not addressed, can emerge to destroy a group (Mindell, 1992).

In management trainings I attended, an organization was often compared to a huge iceberg, with the leaders floating above the water and the workers below supporting the whole organization. Organizational development is dedicated to help the whole iceberg function as a whole. This model, Mindell notes, is insufficient to really explain how things get to be the way they are in organizations, because it leaves out the field. Any model should also include "the influence of the spiritual visions, emotions, feelings, moods and even paranormal events that permeate group life. These invisible influences have been described as dark energy in physics, as the collective unconscious in Jungian psychology, and as a morphogenetic magnetic field in Rupert Sheldrake's concept of the universe" (Ibid., 14).

Mindell notes that in a simple experiment in physics you can put a magnet under a piece of paper and brush metal filings onto the surface of the paper and observe the magnet's force field that organizes the filings. "We think we manage or organize our lives and groups, but actually fields create and organize us as much as we organize them. Fields organize people into groups" (Ibid., 16).

Expressing themselves through values, visions, and beliefs, these invisible fields create group identities. Sometimes fields show up in dreams and in the myths told about a group or a people or a nation. Mindell observes this is why politicians, ecologists, and economists have difficulty dealing with the world:

because it is only partially organized by causal influences.

The world is also organized by the dreaming field. He calls for visionaries and shamans as well as scientists and politicians to address the world's problems. Religious Science describes the field as Intelligence. Earlier peoples understood the wisdom of the world's field, and more than being just wise, the field is the realm of all possibility. We must capture the wisdom and act upon it. We must catch the vision that Higher Intelligence transmits to us.

At the time I directed Forming the Future, I knew nothing about "Time Spirits" or fields. I did know the statement that articulates one of the great laws of our being: "Resist not evil and it will flee from you." Resistance creates a mental image of the thing we fight, which tends to make it more likely that it will manifest.

It is much more effective to look at what we want than to look at what we do not want. Creation Spirituality mystic Ernest Holmes articulated it as "Be for something and against nothing." In addressing chaos, where things are being overturned and confusion appears to be on the surface, it is helpful to remember that just in being for something a great change is taking place, and while on the surface the results may appear a little mixed, underneath a creative power is at work eliminating all unlike itself.

While the voices in the night loomed in my mind, creating trepidation, I opted for another approach. Ultimately, I chose to stay out of fear. I talked it over with the chairman of Forming the Future, and we decided to give the engineer an audience with the executive committee so that his ideas might be fully heard and understood. There was candid discussion, but in the end this plan was not adopted. The full report of the facilities committee, which had the support of all eighty-one schools, was retrieved, and three schools were added back to the list of thirteen originally recommended for funding by the bond issue. They had given their presentations to the large consensual body, but others did not accept a future scenario of population loss due to "white flight."

In retrospect, I think by listening to these ideas we addressed the fears and the energies of despair and, ultimately, racism that existed in the community.

Deidre Combs, in *The Way of Conflict* (2004, 62), uses the image of a spiral that moves through four distinct phases to understand human conflict. She derived this image from her observation of thousands of conflicts and by studying folktales and myths. The first stage begins with a disruption. Here the hero or heroine experiences chaos, challenge, and hopelessness. Then somehow, through a gestalt, the hero figures it out and overcomes the challenge, which enables the return home to stability. If a conflict is not resolved, according to Combs, it will continue on another turn around the dance floor. Combs uses the four elements to describe the spiraling process:

EARTH-DISRUPTION   AIR-STABILITY

WATER-CHAOS   FIRE-CREATIVITY

Following is my interpretation of this event in the context of Comb's model:

Phase 1: Earth – Change and Disruption

The Forming the Future recommendations were in their final phase when the engineer and staff member disrupted the process by developing a totally new model outside the consensus of the facilities committee. I was spun into a state of frenzy. Almost every week the superintendent was pressuring me about the timeline for completion of the project. I felt this disruption might delay our process for months. I was anxious for the process to conclude and had become comfortable with the status quo. The task of disruption is to gather information and ask questions (Ibid., 115). The chairman of Forming the Future and I scheduled hearings before the executive committee so that the engineer could present his information and everyone could ask questions. We did this in a way that honored and respected his work and suspended our disbelief in the data being presented.

Phase 2: Water – Chaos

It seemed we suddenly were wasting hours of time. I expressed my frustration to Willie Kocurek. I had to admire his patience: he seemed unaffected by it all. He proceeded with good humor and willingness to just relax and let the process take its course. This detour became a quick shift of gears instead of a drawn-out nightmare, because we chose not to destroy the opponents or even to be too attached to the previous recommendations of the facilities committee. I felt as if I had fallen into the bottom of a pit again with no escape. Here, in the Water phase, I experienced what Combs describes as follows:

> Depending on the issue, we may feel frustrated and depressed wanting this phase to stop now. The fight or flight reflex really starts kicking in if we feel boxed into a corner. However, believe it or not, this is the richest and most potent time in conflict. (Ibid., 125)

I had lost my perspective. I came up with the idea of getting the chair to intervene with the engineer's employer and assign him to a new project that would take him out of the Forming the Future project. I was going to fight these antics of my colleague and his friend. Water has to flow without impediment, and Willie Kocurek had the wisdom to know this truth, ignoring my desire to get even. I had hit the bottom with my anger and inappropriate approach.

This encounter with conflict helped me let go of my obsolete beliefs and to evolve into a leader with deeper humility. What made me think I was in control anyway? I learned the lesson of flow and tolerance.

Willie Kocurek created an atmosphere of being open to new possibilities. With ample opportunities for expression by all those concerned, I was able to move through the chaos. I grew in my ability to detach from a particular outcome. In this case, all of us were seeking the best possible future for the school district. If indeed the engineer possessed a plan that made more sense, we had to be prepared to detach from our notion that the plan was already completed. We created the space for an opposing view to be heard.

Forgiveness is an action of canceling the expectation that things be a certain way, according to Edith Stauffer in *Unconditional Love and Forgiveness* (1987, 132). In releasing my demand that the engineer be totally content with the recommendations of the facilities committee, I was able to forgive him. I was able to release my anger over this incident.

Open Space Technology developed by Harrison Owen, once an Episcopal priest now turned corporate consultant, provides an interesting insight into how groups of people move and flow. He says meetings are organized by the following (Combs 2004, 140–1):

- Whoever appears are the right people.
- Whatever happens is the only thing that could have happened.
- Whenever it starts is the right time.
- When it's over, it's over.

What great concepts! I could relax and know that this episode, so disturbing at first, was exactly as it was supposed to be. The hearings had incorporated everyone's free will and choices. Instead of forging furiously ahead to meet the superintendent's anxious desire for completion, we stopped to think and reflect once more on the direction we were going. We had been so desirous of Forming the Future and had not realized the power of formlessness.

Phase 3: Fire – Evolution or Creativity

The opposing information got the executive committee to think about whether they held a pessimistic or optimistic view about the community's response to desegregation. I believe everyone remained centered while they captured this new information. I was able to listen and contemplate an alternative plan. I had to focus on a totally new paradigm for how things might be. In the end, the engineer's model of a declining student population did not hold up, but we practiced our listening skills and the engineer felt honored and heard. We went back to our initial plan, passionately committed to building thirteen new schools, not ten.

Phase 4: Air – Stability

The injection of the opposing idea and the subsequent resolution of the conflict by deep listening and questioning and ultimately deciding against the adoption of the innovation brought the executive committee back to a state of equilibrium. Good communication had taken place between the engineer and members of the executive committee. I was able to release all my fears. We had successfully created a win-win method in which we navigated through all four stages to the end. As Combs says, "There are four quarters to the game" (Combs 2004, xxi).

As I am writing about this, I do so from the perspective of one who has a much deeper understanding of conflict. It no longer frightens me as it did in those days. At the time, I felt as though the whole project would be catapulted into a black hole. But this did not happen, and I was initiated into ways of handling conflict effectively for the first time. I learned that I would not die from conflict.

As we listened together, we had to ask the question "Is this true?" Each person on the executive committee asked penetrating questions to the engineer to understand whether the scenario he portrayed was true or not. The committee evaluated the answers and drew a more optimistic conclusion about population growth. It became evident that a diverse group often has greater wisdom for problem solving. At the end of the fourth quarter of the game, the executive committee was solidly on the way to finalizing its conclusions for Forming the Future.

Chapter 11

Passing the Bonds

Once in a while God cuts loose His purse strings,
and gives a big wink to my orchestra.
Hafiz does not require any more prompting than that
to let every instrument inside go berserk.

—Hafiz, *The Gift*

What a journey had been taken with the community as the school board approved the Forming the Future report by a vote on September 11, 1982. The community recommended a $210-million facilities-improvement program and dozens of recommendations for improving the curriculum and programs of the school system. The board wanted to go out for the bond issue in December, but the analysis team felt February would be a better time. In the end, we waited until February. This gave us plenty of time to organize.

As I had done for the main program, I put together a complete handbook for board members and administrators, including responsibilities, timelines, how to disseminate information, media campaign, and do's and don'ts for the bond election. Forming the Future laid the groundwork. The role of the analysis committee of the coordinating council was to determine citizen readiness for the bond issue.

Two polls were commissioned: one five months prior to the bond issue and the second poll one month prior. The first poll indicated the climate created by Forming the Future was positive toward the Austin Independent School District, giving a green light for the bond issue. The second poll was designed to identify respondents who voted in all, in over half, or in no bond elections. It measured voter attitudes about new school buildings, taxes, renovation, quality of life, Forming the Future, the board of trustees, crowded conditions, busing, quality of education, staff, general benefit, growth, after-school use of facilities, and it collected demographic information about respondents. My intuition about including curriculum in the Forming the Future process proved to be correct.

The most important factor on a positive vote for the bonds was the general quality of education (89 percent), the second was the opinion of the teachers/principals (79 percent), the third was crowded conditions in schools (76.6 percent), the opinion of the board of trustees ranked 63 percent, and last was the busing of students (54.2 percent). Some 82.7 percent said that upgrading the school system would be a major step in improving the quality of life in Austin. Some 48.1 percent said they had heard of Forming the Future. Some 57.1 percent agreed that the plan described in Forming the Future represented what the citizens of Austin wanted in their schools. The respondents were fairly evenly distributed across sex, age, and geographical areas; the ethnic categories of respondents were 87.7 percent: white, 7.4 percent black, and 3.7 percent Hispanic.

The poll revealed that good positive groundwork had been laid by Forming the Future, and if an organized bond campaign followed, the outcome would be positive.

Two minor things cropped up. The first was the stance of a prominent businessman who always opposed bond issues. He even advertised against them and posted large signs on a very busy street anytime an issue came up from the city, county, or school district. I went to meet him personally. I told him how much the bonds were needed for the schools. He agreed to support the bonds. Then in an intuitive flash, I got the idea for a commercial. It would star a Mexican American child and this man. The ad began with an eight-year-old Hispanic girl saying "Mr. ____, usually you are not for bonds . . ." to which the man answered, "Yes, Maria, that's generally true.

But this issue is different. New schools are needed, and other schools need repairs. I support these bonds." This was followed by a visual "VOTE FOR THE BONDS FEB. 5, 1983." I wrote the spot and made all the arrangements for the casting. It was considered to be the political coup of the year.

The second interesting event was the sudden appearance in south Austin of literature against the bonds. The information was being distributed by a college student. His mentor was Royal Massett, a man who had actively participated on the finance committee and represented conservative financial interests. I called him up. "Royal, I understand this anti-bond campaign is happening. It's been traced back to you. Why are you doing this? You had every opportunity to shape this process on the finance committee, and as you know these bonds are needed for the schools." There was a long silence. Then Royal responded, "You know, Frances, I've been thinking about taking a little vacation to Mexico." He did, and he disappeared until after the bond issue passed. Without a guide, the young college student's anti-bond campaign folded up, and there was virtually no opposition after that.

These are just a couple of the behind-the-scenes activities I was engaged in during the campaign. I frequently spoke at bond rallies held at schools and was part of the campaign, as were the superintendent and board.

The victory was sweet. The campaign ran like clockwork, with the passage of the bonds by a 4–1 margin on my birthday, February 5, 1983. The election-night celebration included a birthday cake and song of celebration for me. Forming the Future had been a resounding success.

Chapter 12

Passionate Communication

There is no power for change greater than a
community discovering what it cares about.
—Margaret Wheatley, *Turning to One Another and Other:*
Simple Conversations to Restore Hope to the Future

Forming the Future operated on the basis of cocreativity and relationship.

From the beginning there was a commitment on the part of the superintendent and board of trustees to listen to the will of the community. This did not mean having just idle conversations or meetings in the community for the purpose of manipulating public opinion. The community felt they were working for a higher purpose. These elements prevailed:

- conversations in small groups
- consensus building
- conflict management training
- circles
- meetings in large groups
- diversity
- feedback loops for communication among groups
- surveys and polls

- public hearings
- ample time to meet and process information
- a spirit of partnership
- leadership that nurtured the capacities of individuals

The collective was asked to create together a restructured educational system. Given the right conditions, communities can reflect on problems and future possibilities and come up with brilliant solutions. This is spiritual democracy at its best. Howard Gardner, professor at Harvard University, acknowledged:

> Even a combination of fine teachers, exemplary curricula, and powerful, authentic assessments does not in itself suffice. Schools do not operate and probably never have operated in a vacuum. An essential partner in any kind of educational regimen is the community, represented by many individuals ranging from respected elders to powerful business people and officials elected at the local and the national levels. In the United States today, probably the most important agents of change in the community are the parents, in their dual roles as advocates for their children and citizens of society. (Gardner 1991, 255)

Conversations in Small Groups

Most of the meetings in Forming the Future were small groups of under twenty people. Besides the materials provided in appendix A, today there is a plethora of resources to assist organizations in conducting small groups. The links in small groups are a path to a soul-filled society. When the group process and political decision-making get connected, there is a promise of societal change. The plaza and other gathering places become conversation cafes and sacred circles. There are many possible forms the small group process can take to effectively make recommendations for change in organizations, communities, and societies.

Consensus Building

Consensus building was woven into Forming the Future in such a way that the best ideas could be extrapolated from the community. It would be impossible to run the school system on a day-to-day basis by consensus. Forming the Future provided an opportunity for the district decision makers to enter a kind of suspension state for six months and allow the community to come to a consensus about long-range objectives for its public schools. Forming the Future was a true partnership.

Consensus building is largely informal and means having an attitude of welcoming diverse opinions about a proposed course of action. Consensus building is not a dry process but a warm and friendly one. The proposals that are selected are those pretty much everyone can agree on. The key attributes of the leader are respectfulness for people and an ability to listen to differences of opinion on various subjects without attempting to force a specific outcome. The leader empowers others. As a member of the group, the leader also shares opinions but within the give-and-take of the overall process of gaining agreement.

Forming the Future was a participatory process. At the local-school level, in the school-community leadership teams, citizens had to reach agreement on recommendations for improvement. At the district level, committees had to articulate answers to questions and come to a consensus about recommendations to the executive committee, which had the final task of consolidating all the recommendations into a final report. Gaining consensus requires time, but this is a worthwhile investment, because consensus engenders a deep level of commitment. This is not to say that every single committee ceased to exhibit "dominator" behaviors. But by and large, a different leadership environment was created in Forming the Future.

Conflict Management

Individuals who lead small or large groups need to develop conflict-managing skills. Some people will fight for their positions, and this, among many other factors, increases the odds of conflict arising. Fear of conflict creates a reluctance to initiate participatory initiatives. It is easier to make decisions among the staff than to engage the community in the decision-making process. The latter takes more time. Learning about the various individual styles of conflict is helpful (Combs, 2004).

I provided training in conflict management and "thinking on your feet" to the principals. In this way, the school leaders could approach the meetings they would facilitate with greater confidence in their ability to handle the unexpected. I have also found that answering a question with "I don't have the answer to that question, but I would be happy to find out for you" is much more effective than trying to make things up in order to appear knowledgeable or right.

Circles

The executive council of Forming the Future operated as a circle of twenty individuals, nominated to represent both the school-community leadership teams and the coordinating council. Its task was very specific: to refine the recommendations of the entire project, prioritize them, and put them in a report for the board of trustees. However, there were many serious discussions of policy and values in making those determinations. For those who plan similar councils, it is useful to know how other groups organize and listen to one another.

Meetings in Large Groups

Diversity. In Forming the Future, I learned that diversity does not happen naturally. It must be intentional and by invitation. I consciously recruited minority membership to the Forming the Future coordinating council and executive committee. During the time the local school-community leadership teams were meeting, I often visited schools and, like a talent scout, searched for new minority leadership to invite into the district levels of planning.

Feedback loops for communication among groups. Forming the Future provided feedback loops from the school-community leadership teams to the coordinating council committees in the form of written reports summarizing all the data. Likewise, summaries of the actions of the coordinating council were provided back to the schools for their review. Open hearings were also provided as another avenue of communication between the school and district level. This information was summarized for the executive council. The executive council then provided a full report to the board of trustees. Though time-consuming to create, infrequent or absent feedback loops create distance, lack of commitment, and suspicion in people involved in organizations. It's good to err on the side of giving too much information, rather than not providing enough.

Surveys and polls. Forming the Future used surveys of parents at the local school level and political polling at two different times to determine whether or not Forming the Future had penetrated community awareness. This is a good way to gather information from large numbers of people who may not be able to attend a meeting. The polling was conducted by a professional polling firm whose president was involved in Forming the Future by means of random sampling of voters by telephone.

Public hearings. After the local and district recommendation processes ended, public hearings were held to take note of any additional concerns from anyone in the community who wanted to testify, to assure all voices had been heard. These hearings were conducting by members of the coordinating council.

Ample time. Forming the Future was a time-consuming and labor-intensive project. It gave citizens ample time to study, meet, and process information, and to make thoughtful and well-educated recommendations. Today the time could be shortened with the use of the internet. However, there is no substitute for the small-group conversations, which personalized Forming the Future for so many citizens.

Spirit of partnership. A spirit of partnership was created in the community by giving citizens the opportunity to elect delegates to the executive committee and by establishing ground rules, which allowed only one or two staff members on any committee. In this way, the committees were community based, not staff dominated. This was a very important ground rule: it would have been too easy for teachers and administrators to "stack the deck." The purpose of Forming the Future was to listen to the will of the community.

Nurturing leadership. Leadership nurtured the capacities of individuals and trusted the committee heads. It was impossible to control the work of 3,500 people and participate in the work of (ultimately) twenty thousand people who were involved in school-community leadership teams and coordinating council committees, and who completed surveys and attended meetings and public hearings.

(In the back of this book are many resources specific to the discussion in this chapter.)

Chapter 13

Reinventing Education

In doing some historical research on the school district for this book, I found that the district did not contract but grew. In 2005, there were eighty thousand students and 111 schools. Austin ISD placed sixth on the Forbes list of "Best Education in Biggest Cities." In 2004, with strong voter approval, a $519.5-million bond issue was passed. That same year, the district's dynamic superintendent, Pascal Forgione (named in 1999), initiated a yearlong strategic planning effort that obtained input from the general public, district staff, advisory councils, and other stakeholder groups. This, like Forming the Future, though far less comprehensive and community based, provided the public confidence needed to pass the new bond issue.

Ultimately, the values that undergird the educational process have to be reinvented. In 1983, Neal Kocurek noticed there was a need for character education because he was encountering employees, graduates of the system, who had no respect, integrity, or even commitment to their jobs. In his view, their schooling had failed them. Education is the hope for societal change, but today's schools are engaged in teaching to tests and competencies for No Child Left Behind.

When I traveled the country with my husband in 1989/90, we visited over 180 schools in urban, suburban, and rural settings. Stages had been converted into wrestling areas, and most of the arts programs had disappeared. Libraries had encyclopedias over twenty years old and very poor book selections. It seemed as though education had taken a turn downward. We saw only a handful of well-run schools. How can education be reinvented and infused with new life?

I think the reinvention of education has to begin by determining the values we wish to instill in our youth. This was a missing piece for me in the Forming the Future project. If I were to do it again, I would add a piece in which the community looked at core values and whether or not the schools were promoting values that supported a community vision of what would be needed for the future.

Neal Kocurek had the vision to recommend character education for the schools that are part of the AWE project. A well-constructed values component for Forming the Future might elicit many of the values that are integrated here, from creativity to ecology, from courage to critical thinking, from community to awe.

I am impressed with the AWE project initiated by Matthew Fox. It includes ancestral- and wisdom-based education, and injects the ten Cs to balance the three Rs of reading, writing, and arithmetic. The ten Cs are (Fox 2006, 104–143):

1. Cosmology and Ecology
2. Contemplation, Meditation
3. Creativity
4. Chaos and Darkness
5. Compassion
6. Courage
7. Critical Consciousness and Judgment
8. Community
9. Ceremony, Celebration, and Ritual
10. Character and Chakra Development

The program Fox has developed is an after-school project from 3:00 to 6:00 p.m., Monday through Thursdays, and is being piloted in Oakland, California. It begins with a half hour of *chi gung* or yoga, followed by homework assistance, then the teaching of the day, which includes new cosmology or ecological awareness or the mysteries of nature, with the final hour dedicated to putting the teachings of the day into creative expression of rap poetry, video, drumming, painting, creating comic books, and more (Ibid., 155). Rather than a frontal attack that threatens the schools, this after-school program of three more hours promises to educate mind and soul. The project is very exciting. It could guide innovative spiritual curriculum in churches as well.

Without broader participation, however, AWE will be relegated to just another pilot program and not impact the broader educational system. Imagine how powerful AWE might be if combined with an empowerment process in which the community and school system come to accept the values of this project and actively work to see these principles included in school practice and pedagogy.

David Wilcox describes five levels of participation that offer increasing degrees of control to a community, starting with the least involvement:

1. **Information**
   The least you can do is tell people what is planned.

2. **Consultation**
   Offer a number of options and listen to the feedback you get.

3. **Deciding together**
   Encourage others to provide additional ideas and options, and to join in deciding the best way forward.

4. **Acting together**
   Different interests decide together what is best and form a partnership to carry it out.

5. **Supporting independent community initiatives**
   Help others do what they want—perhaps within a framework of grants, advice, and support provided by the resource holder.

(Wilcox n.d., 199)

Forming the Future used all these levels but mostly operated at the fourth level. Four models are commonly used for planning within organizational systems. The *traditional model* is top-down, with fairly rigid steps and little room for meaningful stakeholder participation. The *legislative model* is used to guide and direct the decisions of an organization's governing body. The administrative staff is actively involved in the model and often uses the community to gain "buy-in" or legitimize decisions made by the community's governing body. In the *limited community participation* model, the process is initiated by a governing body, a citizens committee is involved for ten to eighteen months, and after a report to the governing body, the activities are internalized to the decision-making processes of the administrative team or governing body.

The *community empowerment process* model was used in Forming the Future and is built around extensive community participation over a long period of time. The process is initiated by a proactive governing body, the school board and superintendent. An institutionalized process to ensure continued citizen participation is established. A process is created to monitor progress toward goals. The process to ensure continued citizen participation was at first somewhat truncated and then discontinued.

There are many traits associated with leadership styles of the two basic strategic-planning processes:

Traditional Management	**Empowerment Management**
Expert learners	Open learners
Coalition builders	Consensus builders
Controlling	Facilitating
Manipulative	Empowering
Directing	Sharing
Goal focused	Goal negotiable
Assertive/aggressive	Flexible/permissive
Filtered accessibility	Accessible
Information filters	Information disseminators
Impatient	Patient/tolerant

The results of the project were heartwarming, but had the close partnership continued even more good could have been accomplished. Deep democracy takes time and commitment. It is rarely expedient.

In 1985, a full evaluative report was made by the department of research and evaluation of the Austin Independent School District (*The Future Revisited: A Progress Report on Forming the Future*). The report summarized progress on eighty-eight propositions and 292 related recommendations: approximately 86 percent were in progress or completed, 9 percent were designated for future action, and 5 percent were found to be either unfeasible or unnecessary. Major educational progress included provision of computers, programs for gifted and talented, programming on cable television, a longer elementary school day, magnet schools, expanded offerings in science, health, and foreign languages, programs for the handicapped, texts for learning-disabled students, and an improved discipline policy. Major progress was made on nine community involvement goals. Major progress in resource management included lower pupil-teacher ratio, approval of school bonds, and various facilities improvements.

For a number of years, a committee chaired by Willie Kocurek, the former citizen chair of Forming the Future, continued to monitor the progress of the district toward the goals. By and large, as the evaluation report reveals, what was recommended was accomplished, and in record time. Since then, there has not been a cooperative effort between the Austin Independent School District and the Austin community of this scale. Forming the Future was a unique collaboration. The complete organizational format of the project may be found in appendices A and B.

Part III

The Spiritual Underpinnings

Chapter 14

Powerful Intentions

Because spirit is infinite, or limitless, it is everywhere and therefore
it follows that the whole of spirit must be present at every point
in space at the same moment. All spirit is concentrated at any
point in space that we may choose to fix our thought upon.
—Thomas Troward, *The Edinburgh Lectures*

The nineteenth-century judge and metaphysical writer Thomas
Troward had a notion of the power of intention. It is the idea that love,
life, God, and energy are everywhere present, and because *it* is being all
things, *it* is also being you. The extent to which you are selective about
which intentions you put out to the field will determine how things unfold.
The "field" to Troward and to his successor, Ernest Holmes, was predicated
to be a creative medium that operated as a spiritual law. The quality of
the word calls the law into action. To speak the word we must have a
foundation that we are unified with all life. "That our future destiny is to
actually take an individual part, however small, in guiding the great work
of Evolution may not be evident to us in the earlier stages of our awakening"
(Troward 1917, 179).

Life is undifferentiated in itself, and our individual differentiation of this
energy depends on our recognition of it. Thus, the field is undifferentiated
potential until it is differentiated by an individual personality. In this

sense, no person can come "to the Father" or the Parent Spirit except through the Son (John 14:6).

If I want to attend a class in Chartres for Wisdom University, the first movement in that direction is my thought or desire. I have to manifest money for the trip and reserve my airline ticket, but as far as my intention is concerned, I am already there. It is the Word, Thought, or Desire of the individualized Spirit that localizes its activity in a definite center. Intention is the key to the relationship between the Field (the Law) and the individual. Well, then what is the Word? How do I pick the right words to use?

Some have called the Word the "Secret Name of God" or "the lost word." Jesus used the Word to proclaim healings. The idea is that every external fact has a spiritual origin. The outer phenomenon has a corresponding inward principle or *noumenon*, which derives from the Latin word *nomen*, meaning "name." Thus, there is a hidden name to all things. The specific words we use do not matter. What does matter is the faith and intention with which we use them.

We create a spiritual prototype with our conception or thought. This is intention. *Intention* contains the word "tent" within it. It is as though we take a concept into our innermost tent of consciousness and give it our thought, and this energy of concentrated attention connects with the Field or Law.

Rupert Sheldrake, a British biologist, developed a hypothesis of formative causation, which states that the forms of self-organizing living things, from molecules to galaxies, are shaped by morphic fields that have a resonance or cumulative memory of similar systems through time and culture (Sheldrake 1981). Species remember how to look and behave because of these fields. The fields act more like habits than laws and can be modified. Other physicists have suggested how this might be possible.

William Tiller, professor emeritus at Stanford University, an expert in the fields of metallurgy and solid state physics, has also published more than ninety papers in the area of psychoenergetics. In his early writings in the seventies, Tiller theorized that intention operates as its own dimension. He found in a materialistic scientific paradigm there was no place where human consciousness, intention, emotion, mind, or spirit could enter. At the same time, Tiller found abundant data that showed humans can have a significant effect on physical reality. "Matter as we know it is hardly a fragrance of a whisper" (Tiller n.d.).

While subject to the criticism of his colleagues at Stanford, Tiller continued to do conventional research on crystallization to keep his day job while pursuing his passion on researching how the universe is constructed (Adams n.d.). Most recently, thanks to private grants, Tiller has been able to document the effects of human intention. His book *Conscious Acts of Creation: The Emergence of a New Physics* describes this work (Tiller, Dibble, and Cohane 2001). Tiller believes we have a layered reality, a bio-body suit made of four layers:

> The outermost layer is the electric monopole substance layer—that's our conventional world. The first inner layer is magnetic monopole substance layer—that's the coarsest layer of the vacuum. It's another part of physical reality. The next inner layer is the emotion domain substance layer. And the fourth inner layer is the mind domain substance layer. This is like a kind of diving bell. There's a portion of our spirit self inside this device. The spirit activates the device through intention. (Ibid., 5)

Tiller says that although we appear to be separated from one another, at the first inner layer level we are all connected.

Einstein worked on an equation between mass and energy found in the relationship $e=MC2$. Tiller finds there is another part of the equation, which is energy converting back and forth to human consciousness into love.

Divine Love, from the level of spirit, creates everything. It goes to consciousness, and consciousness goes to energy, and energy goes to matter. This is how intention from the level of spirit can influence the substance of the outer layer of the bio-body suit, and that aspect of the world. As we increase, through intention, the coupling between the outermost layer and the first inner layer, we increased the magnitude of the effect. If the effect becomes big enough, we totally change the world" (Ibid., 9).

What an exciting concept! If, as a mass of people, we increase through an intention of Forming the Future, we increase the magnitude of the connection as well as the effect. Tiller's view of the Big Bang is that before the Big Bang there was spirit, the mind domain, and the emotion domain. Divine intention created the Big Bang and formed the layers of the body suit. We have to learn to develop the gift of intentionality with our exercise of free choice. Coming home for Tiller is when we are able to experience that total coherence of all life.

David Bohm, writing in *Wholeness and the Implicate Order* (1980), says that all ordering influence and information is contained in the invisible domain and can be called upon in times of need. Lynne McTaggart, in *The Field: The Quest for the Secret Force of the Universe* (2001), describes dozens of studies supporting the existence of an energy dimension or field of intention that can be used by everyone. Ernest Holmes noted, "How much of this Infinite Good is ours? ALL OF IT! And how much of It may we have to use? AS MUCH OF IT AS WE CAN EMBODY" (1926, 50).

There is no single locus of intention. It is built into the universe and everywhere present. The key is understanding the reciprocal relationship between people and people, as well as between the universe and all sentient beings. Thomas Troward said, "Order was the first principle of the universe." In living systems there is a drive for greater coherence; there is communication between the individual and the Field and vice versa. This intelligent field that connects everything in creation has been called "The Matrix" by the father of quantum physics, Max Planck. It is also called "The Divine Matrix" or "The Divine Mother." Ernest Holmes called it the "Universal Soul" or "Universal Anima." It is the sum total of all creation as well as the link between our inner world of thoughts and feelings and the outer world of what we believe to be beyond our bodies. The Universal Soul mirrors in the outer world what we create in our beliefs.

The Gospel of Thomas also presents a message from Jesus that says, "If you bring forth what is inside you, what you have will save you. If you do not have that within you, what you do not have within you will kill you" (Lynch 1998, 257, "Logoin 70").

What is inside us is the creative intention of the Divine Matrix. We must allow ourselves to be in harmony with the Source of all wisdom and bring it in to action on the physical plane.

"Isn't it an interesting thing to stop and consider without splitting one's personality that there could be something in me with which I am so intimately related that it is what I am, which is transcendent, emanating from a supreme source, forever one with the eternal heart of God and the eternal mind and intelligence in the universe—so that everyone could say this and believe it and use it every day?" (Holmes 2007).

The goals of Forming the Future were in and of themselves powerful intentions designed to unify the collective community around a vision for the improved education of children. My intention was to be the instrument by which this was accomplished.

Jesus knew about this, as he said, "If two of you agree down here on Earth concerning anything you ask for, my Father in Heaven will do it for you." To agree is to vibrate together in phase, in quantum correlation.

Another way to look at intention is the way Sri Aurobindo did in *The Divine Life* (1939) when he said that people who aligned their will to the divine will had the ability to explore a new realm of creativity beyond the laws of science. The alignment takes place by suspending an attachment to the sensory world and becoming open to a higher consciousness.

Goswami says you could imagine a possibility cloud of consciousness with myriad transcendent potential, which interfaces with humans and between human minds: "Consciousness mediates the transfer of electronic potentia from one brain to another" (Goswami 2001, 39).

Psychologist William Braud explored the influence of individual intention on other living things (McTaggert 2001, 128–139). Initially, he calculated the velocity of a gerbil on its run and experimented to see if human intention could make it go faster. Once he proved this, he launched experiments on the effects of being stared at. From his studies, Braud concluded that people had some means of communicating and responding to remote attention. Similar experiments have been conducted by Rupert Sheldrake.

Braud found some practices guaranteed success in increasing telepathy and awareness:

- Those who relaxed to reduce left brain function through meditation, biofeedback, or other method, accessed information of a different quality.

- Those who believe that intention works get better results.
- Those who believed in everything as an interconnected whole were more likely to have an experience.
- Those who believed there were other ways to communicate other than through accepted channels.

The German word *Ganzfeld* means "whole field." This whole field, or what Ernest Holmes called the "Universal Mind," can be used by ordinary people to heal others. An intention for health can create an improved order and suggests that illness is a disturbance in the quantum fluctuations of an individual. Intention involves overlapping realities.

The six-pointed star, two overlapping triangles pointing in opposite directions, symbolizes the intersection of human intention with the field. In the Kabbalah, it is called the "Star of David." It represents a person whose consciousness has reached higher levels. Sometimes there is an encounter with Emptiness, Nothingness, and Silence. It is where we may find an infinite number of quanta, or bits and pieces, that make up sets of possibilities for almost anything to happen.

Prayer is another form of intention. Jesus said, "Where two or more are gathered in my name, there am I in the midst of them" (Matt. 18:15–20). There is only one Presence: Love, Life, God, Energy, whatever you choose to call it. This One is present, intelligent, and omni-available. There is a dimension of intention in the universe that takes your vision, your belief, and thought, and projects it into form. Jesus expressed this as "It is done unto you as you believe" (Matt. 9:29).

I am reminded of the 1997 Italian film *La Vita è Bella* (*Life is Beautiful*), which tells the story of Guido Orefice, a Jew, who uses his fertile imagination to help his son survive their internment in a Nazi concentration camp. Guido's intention is to spare his son the pain and suffering of the camp, and he convinces the boy that the camp is a game in which the first person to get a thousand points wins a tank. He tells his son that all the other children are hiding to win the game because that is the way they win points. As the Americans are drawing near, Guido instructs his son to stay in a sweatbox until everybody has left. Little Giosue manages to survive and thinks he has won the game when an American tank arrives to liberate the camp. He is then reunited with his mother, Dora.

Intention accesses a different way of knowing. I knew a developer in Austin who used unconventional means to discover his projects. He was in the business of remodeling run-down shopping malls. To determine if a project was worthy, he would go to the site and spend the night there. He said that when he would wake up the next day he would "know" whether or not to do it. He could sense an emerging future between himself and the piece of property.

In the book *Presence*, Joseph Jaworski developed a theory of different levels of perception and change, using a "U" to distinguish different depths of perception (Senge, Scharmeir, Jaworski, and Flowers 2005). Jaworski describes three stages: observe, observe, observe, become one with the world; "retreat and reflect" allow the inner knowing to emerge, "act swiftly, with a natural flow." The three stages are called sensing, presencing, and realizing, as the chart below shows:

sensing   **realizing**

U

presencing

The authors of *Presence* note that

> the state at the bottom of the U is presencing, seeing from the deepest source and becoming a vehicle for that source. When we suspend and redirect our attention, perception starts to arise from within the living process of the whole. When we are presencing, it moves further, to arise from the highest future possibility that connects self and whole. The real challenge in understanding presencing lies not in its abstractions but in the subtlety of the experience. (Ibid., 89)

Forming the Future was informed by a larger intention. It was infused with who I was and my purpose in being alive. It was not about getting votes for a bond issue; it was about creating some amazing conversations and synergy with the community to create better schools.

What I came to know in doing Forming the Future: our natural state of being is a relationship, and there is a drive toward greater communication and coherence. We are in communion with the Field, are enriched by it, and draw from it. How we form our future depends upon our interaction with the Field. The more elegant and purposeful the intention, the greater the universal response. The reciprocity of Spirit is demonstrated through the power of intention.

Chapter 15

Visioning

The presence of grass stains on a calling does not
immediately disqualify it from the running.

—Gregg Levoy

Visioning is not brainstorming. It is not visualization. It is not
"imagineering." It involves surrender, relaxing into the stillness, and
emptying the mind so that a higher vision may emerge. It is more akin to
pondering or active contemplation. We release all the chatter in our minds,
the constantly moving thoughts, and become truly quiet. Visioning is like
taking a mini-retreat to the woods where we may listen and wait for an
emergence of what is to come.

Ernest Holmes said, "There comes to each the logical and exact result
of his own receptivity. To each, life brings the reward of his own visioning"
(1926, 442).

"Dreams come in the interest of our greater well-being," Jeremy Taylor
often emphasizes in his workshops. Some people do not have dreams but
experience waking dreams or visions. A variety of intuitional phenomena
may occur at this level as the soul's way of visioning. Teresa of Avila
describes some of the subtle phenomena in her master work *The Interior
Castle* (Teresa of Avila, 1588). These may occur as sound, understanding,
archetypes, images, and subtle intuitions.

Tapping into the Universal Mind is one of the outcomes of visioning, a state of meditation where we become receptive to the Divine Pattern of Perfection underlying all creation. When we are able to "catch" the vision in our mind's eye, we can create a mental equivalent or develop intentions for accomplishing what is revealed in the visioning. Michael Beckwith says,

> Visioning is a process by which we train ourselves to be able to hear, feel, see and catch God's plan for our life or for any particular project we're working on. An organic process that has evolved for me as I grow spiritually, it is based on the idea that we're not here to tell God what to do or to ask God for things but to absolutely be available for what God is already doing, to open ourselves up to catch what's already happening. My initial discoveries more than twenty years ago on my spiritual path allowed me to see that there is a bigger pattern of life, a level of reality beyond the mere human experiential life. These awarenesses shifted my perception tremendously and the visioning process developed as a way of applying that new insight. (Juline1996)

The practice of visioning or sitting for an idea yielded most of the formative ideas for Forming the Future. Vision comes from a connection with the field of all possibility. When a deep state of stillness or emptiness is obtained, there is an opportunity to communicate with the divine. Deep ideas emerge from this state, without the limitations of the conscious mind. At the beginning of Forming the Future, I was given one month to come up with a design for the project. Sitting alone in my office, I practiced visioning, emptying my mind of everything and just sitting for an idea.

Not every visioning session will yield forms or direction. Visions develop over time in an organic way. It's more like Emerson's view of "getting our bloated nothingness out of the way of the divine circuits." We simply allow vision to happen and get out of the way. It is important to note that visions, like callings, often are a little murky and grass stained. This does not disqualify them. Visions can be unsettling and mysterious.

They do not automatically lead you to a yellow notepad for writing out the action plan.

Any person can use visioning as a way of bringing the Universal Mind into an experience of creating life. Visioning is nothing more than listening to higher Intelligence.

Visioning for a Specific Purpose

Visioning can be used to pose a question to the infinite mind about anything: an event, an organization, a project, a retreat, or one's life. It can be done by an individual or in a group. Recently, I used a visioning group to create a retreat. In a group, wisdom comes from more than one person. Visioning as a group provides a space of deep listening to hear Spirit's highest vision or idea for a project.

Visioning recognizes there is one cosmic reality principle that is infinite in nature and the substance of all things. When it is used to begin an endeavor, guidance from the Center of Life is requested, listened to, and honored. When an individual or a group of individuals visions for something, they commit to surrender their human knowing and experience, so they may listen to the guiding and sacred voice of Spirit for "what wants to happen."

Visioning before setting goals, making plans, and implementing changes allows for the world of possibilities to come into play. People, although perhaps highly skilled in planning, strategizing, or creating success, may be limited by their experiences when it comes to entertaining what might be something more exquisite than they already know. Visioning initiates a journey into the unknown to access that which is beyond our human knowing.

Visioning brings forth the calling from the heart, clarifying desire, passion, purpose, or direction for moving forward. This provides a path for effective action. In a group, visioning brings forth the deepest listening of all persons involved and provides an ear and voice for all participants so each knows more fully what the commitment is. It is a genesis that boosts the team's spirit, gives direction, and increases effectiveness. Visioning allows us to consider a project's alignment with a higher purpose.

After visioning, a project often tends to develop effortlessly, with a higher degree of accountability. My visioning for Forming the Future created the model of the entire project in the form of a picture of all the component parts, on a timeline. On the other hand, a project may also dissolve as it is discovered that the idea does not have the necessary ownership or "what wants to happen" is something else.

Generally, visioning is done until there is clarity about the direction of a project. If the project is already scheduled, then visioning can be used to flesh out the conceptual frameworks of an event or project. Sometimes participants see vague images and not in concrete terms. The questions I asked were the following:

1. What is the perfect idea for Forming the Future?
2. What does the organization look like?
3. What must be released?
4. What information do I need, in this moment, to get started?

Visioning brings into the present a future potential. In the process of visioning, we become aware of a future seeking to emerge. It is not just *some* future but the highest future available to a human being. It is not a future someone else has created for us, but one that is intimately connected with our Self.

Mihaly Csikszentmihalyi says that if we want to direct evolution we must not only look at genes but at memes:

> It is essential to remember that every time we invest attention in an idea, a written word, a spectacle; every time we purchase a product; every time we act on a belief; the texture of the future is changed, even if in microscopic ways. The world in which our children and their children will live is built, minute by minute, through the choices we endorse with our psychic energy. (Csikszentmihalyi 1993, 165)

Visioning adds value and intelligence about ideas, projects, areas of concern. It is a spiritual activity in that it accesses a way of wisdom. As our visions become clarified, our spiritual evolution requires that we act for a harmonious future. We must not just seek our personal ideas, but we must seek transcendent ideas that are part of the collective well-being of all life, the stream of evolution that will form the future and influence a matrix for a new wisdom civilization.

Chapter 16

Open at the Top

All channels are free and all doors fly open for my
immediate and endless, Divinely Designed supply.
—Florence Scovell Shinn, *Your Word Is Your Wand*

When I hear the expression "open at the top," I think of a container without a lid. I read somewhere that a bumble bee, if dropped into an open tumbler, will be there until it dies, unless it is taken out. It never sees the means of escape at the top but tries to find its way out through the sides near the bottom. It will seek a way until it completely destroys itself. In many ways, the term "open at the top" is a reality that is difficult to accept. We often struggle with problems and concerns without ever recognizing that the solutions are open and available to us when we shift perspective.

Ernest Holmes taught that everyone should be "open at the top" in regard to their religion, which he viewed as an evolving work in progress. In a biography written after his death, his brother Fenwicke cited Holmes's expressed opinion that all beliefs are valid to those who hold them. He thought that new revelations were constantly happening and it was important to be open to the new rather than locked into specific dogmas or doctrines that bind one to the past. "Open at the top" means open to the process of spiritual revelation on a day-to-day basis.

It is also an expression of willingness to be flexible in the design of a project, to be accepting of diversity, to be welcoming of the untested and new. It was one of the characteristics of Forming the Future that *anyone* could create a committee to address a need believed to be important, provided a group of people could be formed who were interested in that problem.

"Open at the top" also implies there is a level of reality beyond the five senses in which we participate. Our top is the crown chakra, a level of higher awareness or relationship to the divine. When we open to our intuition, the undefined can become defined, randomness can take on a pattern, and we are guided to cocreate in harmony with the whole. "Open at the top" implies a willingness to dwell in silence and listen to Spirit for answers. When we directly perceive truth through intuition, we are provided deeper insights that are richer than thought. These intuitions need to be developed further by reason and formulated more fully with words. As our thought expands, we gain greater understanding and begin to attract people, information, capacities, books, inventions, and communications that will enhance our potential to evolve. Intuition is not dictatorial, does not demand. It invites us to consider. Intuition happens most often when we are "open at the top."

The intuitive part of Forming the Future was in creating a flexible organizational chart, which would be modified with the input from the community. The chart seemed to organize itself from the voices in the community. In Forming the Future, everyone was invited to share what was of concern to them. There was also an open invitation to the business community to participate in the process. Any person who called my office seeking to participate was interviewed by staff and placed on a committee of their choice or on a committee they wanted to create. What began as only ten committees evolved into over thirty-four different work groups.

That is how a personnel committee was formed, which was staffed with personnel experts from companies all over the city. In their study of the personnel department, the committee discovered that the district was using antiquated personnel software and procedures. This committee helped the staff by recommending streamlined personnel practices.

Information came in so fast. It was a matter of accommodation and being willing to have a different relationship to the future. It was about trusting that there is an intelligence that reveals itself through all participants. It was about vision and intention. There was a larger purpose behind Forming the Future: how do we serve the higher idea of educating our children for the future? Each and every person is an instrument for something better to emerge.

When I am willing to surrender my will to control the organization and destiny of a project, and work in harmony with the will of the community, I open to a dimension that is beyond description. When I am open at the top, I am in service of the universe, and no longer just of my limited individual concept of how it should be. I embrace the new. I am creating a vacuum that can be filled. I am alluring the open-ended future. I often joke that I am open to a download from the infinite. Shifting the personal story from *Catcher in the Rye* to "Catcher of the Infinite Wisdom" is a much more fulfilling way to live my life.

On a very practical level, I am open to whole networks of communication through the internet. I can access information and research, find almost any person through national directories. I am also open to other information. A few months ago, I was contemplating doing a project with someone, and shrill voices went off inside my head shouting "No!" I had to back off from the project. I neither think of myself as a player upon a stage, full of sound and fury, nor as a victim of circumstance, but more as a cocreator, involved in the development of the world. The freedom I find in using cyberspace as well as the joy of receiving personal revelations from Universal Mind have made me even more reluctant to live by decree. Fundamentalism— the notion that our world is completely ordained and we must follow the rules—does not fit an open-at-the-top worldview.

Of course, Spirit is a part of all this. It's just that there are many possibilities in God. In chaos theory, the flapping of a butterfly's wings can cause a hurricane halfway around the world. The internet teaches us to see the value of diversity and plurality. All opinions of all people matter. The one path, one story, one approach to God that fundamentalism teaches is fast becoming obsolete. The only way forward is to be "open at the top." We are the network, and it includes all dimensions. Therein lies its power, the hope of humanity for a better future.

Chapter 17

The Creative Process

Forming the Future used the creative process. At its highest level, it was a divine ideal about a better school system. There was an involution of the ideal into the body politic, into the people of Austin, Texas (Via Positiva). The new ideal disturbed the status quo. Then there was chaos, in which hundreds of people participated in making choices and imagining what education could be in their local schools (Via Negativa). Afterwards the ideas began to take form into a set of recommendations for creative action (Via Creativa). Finally, changes were embraced and carried out (Via Transformativa).

There are several models that show how the mind works in the creative process. Ernest Holmes envisions a circle representing Universal Spirit subdivided into three parts: spirit, soul, and body. Human thought, being creative, acts as creator and moves an idea into the creative medium of soul, which attracts all the elements necessary to form that thought into action or effect.

The individual spirit is microcosm to a macrocosm and accesses higher consciousness in the creation of all forms.

The Italian Roberto Assagioli (1888–1974), founder of psychosynthesis, developed an egg diagram to describe the relationships of various parts of the self to the Self and to the Universal Soul or Collective Unconscious. The egg itself is drawn with a dotted line, suggesting the diaphanous relationship between the universal and the particular. Assagioli's original egg depicted the point of contact with the Higher Self as being at the top of the diagram. In a modification of the chart by John Firman and Ann Russell, the Higher Self, similar to the U Movement, is reached not only in the heights of bliss (Via Positiva) but also in the depths (Via Negativa). The second egg diagram, therefore, has the Higher Self located at both the top *and* bottom. The Higher Self can also be considered the *Deep Self*—at the very core of our consciousness and being. Both depictions of the egg diagram are shown below.

Two Depictions of the Egg Diagram

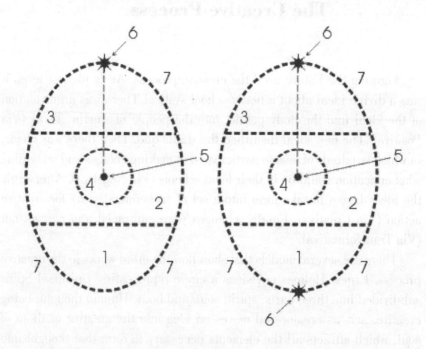

Parts of Assagioli's Egg Diagram

1. The Lower Unconscious
2. The Middle Unconscious
3. The Higher Unconscious or Superconscious
4. The Field of Consciousness
5. The Conscious Self or "I"

6. The Higher Self
7. The Collective Unconscious

1. The Lower (Infra) Unconsciousness

The unconscious drives and instincts are stored in this part of our psyche. Much of what unconsciously motivates our acting and thinking has its ground here, including repressed thoughts and feelings. Far removed from our field of conscious awareness, this enables us to be in a waking state unbothered by fears, grief, and anxieties. The Lower Unconsciousness is where pathology takes root. (Perhaps this is hell.)

2. The Middle Unconsciousness

This part of the unconscious can be accessed during our waking state. It is an intermediate state between waking and sleeping.

3. The Higher Unconsciousness

Artistic and scientific intuition are part of this field of genius and altruism. This field in consciousness is only rarely accessible for most people.

4. The Field of Consciousness

This part of our personality is available to us during the waking state as an endless stream of images, sensations, thoughts, feelings, desires, and impulses that we can observe and analyze.

5. The Conscious Self or Ego

The center of our consciousness is represented by the black dot in the diagram. From here we observe, regulate, and judge the content of our consciousness. Much like the driver of a car, the conscious self controls everything going on in the vehicle of consciousness. It is the "I" of us that has a name.

6. The Higher Self

When we sleep, our self, or conscious I, seems to be lost. When we awake and come to our senses, we regain our consciousness again. This Self is responsible for keeping alive all our involuntary functions, both biological and psychological. Wherever we have a feeling of "I-ness," it is grounded in something higher. This Self is permanent and not affected by the daily flow of consciousness or by the physical process of our body, but can be experienced as the Source of our consciousness. Kant called it the *noumenal ego,* as distinguished from the empirical ego. (This could be heaven.)

Assagioli's intention was for psychology to be a science that could integrate all the different functions of the human psyche into a whole. The Self had the highest potential to bring about this harmony. Thus, his therapy built the whole structure of the personality around a concept of the Higher Self using all its potential to unify individual consciousness. By integrating fully the energies of the Higher Self, a true synthesis is achieved. Assagioli named his new psychology *psychosynthesis.*

7. The Collective Unconsciousness

In the egg diagram, consciousness reaches the collective consciousness through osmosis (represented by a dotted line). This overall consciousness is termed the collective unconsciousness because most people are not conscious of the fact that they are embedded in this larger field of consciousness. By introducing the concept of the Higher Self into Western psychology, Assagioli opened it up to transpersonal realms now being explored by Ken Wilber and others.

Assagioli based psychosynthesis on esoteric psychology and the work of Alice Bailey, a theosophical scholar. He developed techniques for obtaining a spiritual psychosynthesis to attain harmony and bliss in the human psyche. He believed there is a natural tendency in the human psyche to reach for higher forms of consciousness. The ego wants to come into contact with its own Source of Being. The Self, out of its own nature, wants us to be lifted up. This relationship can be described in religious, psychological, or artistic language. Like Ernest Holmes, Assagioli asserted that the correspondence between macrocosm and microcosm *works*, whether you know why it happens or not.

Human beings feel the call or the pull of the line, and this pulling force can be beneficial. It is in the nature of the psyche to always reach higher and beyond. This reaching is already healthy. Assagioli developed techniques to reinforce the pulling of the line. Some of them include (1) using spiritual archetypes and symbols; (2) visualizing an inner teacher with whom the student could dialogue and gain guidance; (3) the dramatization of a spiritual quest, using great spiritual stories such as the legend of the Holy Grail or scenes from Dante's *Divine Comedy*. Through role-playing, the student would undergo the same problems and the same catharsis as the characters they were enacting.

The conscious self exists within a field of consciousness that accesses all the other levels. This model clearly establishes the idea of panentheism, "All there is, is in God," in contrast to pantheism which says "It is all God." The latter clearly establishes that inclusion is not synonymous with identity. Creation Spirituality is panentheistic also. Jesus said, "The Father within me doeth the work" (John 14:10). The diaphanous egg shows the correspondence of the individual with the universal consciousness. To the extent that we can become more open to the Original Creative Intelligence, we can exercise more creative power as individuals. All life interfaces with universal consciousness and is in some sense cocreative. Panentheism would cause us to realize that our own power of creativity has its origin in an All-originating Mind. As long as we maintain a connection with this Mind, it acts as a multiplier.

The circulation between Mind and the individual produces an endless flow of life, expanding in love, power, joy, and intelligence. This can only happen when the individual recognizes his creative powers are in harmony with Spirit.

What creates separation and lack of flow are inversions—emotional and mental aspects of ourselves that have not been healed, which adulterate the stream of life and creativity. When the lower unconscious (1) is filled with repressed material (anger, fear, and hatred), this becomes the focus of the mind and causes an inversion, blocking our access to the Higher Self or mediating experience. In extreme cases, the messages sent to the Higher Self are of hate, fear, and anger, and result in a misuse of the universal intelligence. This is why many years of study and preparation of consciousness are part of most religious systems of the world.

Rabbi Heschel says that God is "the most (and best) moved mover." Along these lines of thought, human creativity enriches experience, including the Divine Life itself. When we recognize that by our choices we can contribute something to the glory of God, rather than being able to add nothing to God, it gives new meaning to all that we do. We get to serve the Infinite not just as a means to our personal ends but as a significant contribution to the Divine Life, to the greater good of all. This is flow at its best. Forming the Future engaged these energies of contribution to the greater whole.

The flow experience occurs when there are clear goals with feedback and when the challenge is balanced by skill level. The person in flow state experiences a merging of action and awareness in the present moment, both with a sense of control and loss of self-consciousness. It is a timeless state of mind where the activity becomes autotelic (Csikszentmihalyi 1990, 54–70). A counter-force of "psychic entropy," a disorder in consciousness: bad moods, ennui, lack of motivation, inability to focus, can take over consciousness and disrupt flow. Flow is a way to evolve both personally and culturally. To sustain flow, new challenges must be taken on to create an upward spiral of complexity. We have to self-surpass our past to form the future.

Flow occurs when individuals are gathered as a group, in oneness of mind, in agreement, resulting in a multiplication of energy around an intention. This is the creative process used by a group. In Forming the Future, people were also presented with complexity, with a new challenge of determining what they wanted to see in their schools. They were given the opportunity to surpass the status quo.

Alfred North Whitehead defined creativity as "the universal of universals characterizing legitimate matter of fact. It is that ultimate principle by which the many, which are the universe disjunctively, become the one actual occasion, which is the universe conjunctively. It lies in the nature of things that the many enter into complex unity" (Whitehead 1978, 21).

When intuition breaks through to a greater unity, it moves into a field beyond time and space. As we have been open at the top, we connect to a much vaster God or Universal Spirit and thus powerful creative force. Thomas Troward said we had to see ourselves as a center of Divine Operation, at the heart of the creative process. We have to find a larger self than the one that lives in a limited, physical body. God has given us access to the entire cosmos, including the dark matter and unformed substance. As cocreators, we are citizens of the universe and absolutely without limitation.

God is present in the very midst of our forming the future, offering new possibilities in every moment for the highest outcome. If God is creative, and God is love, then there is an allurement taking place in which everyone is being led, urged, enticed, persuaded—but never forced—to greater depths and heights of creativity and joy.

Roberto Assagioli was the first Western psychologist to seriously incorporate religion and spirituality into an overall view of the human psyche. Freud considered all forms of religion and spirituality to be a regression into childlike states of consciousness. Carl Jung, a student of Freud, disagreed with the old master and held a more positive view about the role religion played in the human psyche. Jung discovered universal symbols at work in the unconscious, which he called "archetypes." They were unconscious images of certain psychological realities, charged with tremendous psychodynamic energy, like the image of the archetypical mother who would always look after you or of the white horse as a symbol of freedom. Jung studied these symbols and tried to unravel the secrets of the unconscious. Archetypes are like batteries filled with high energy, able to ignite the psyche into lofty goals and aspirations, and images of a better human being, a better world. They are images of the Self, the higher part of the psyche. Jung did not make a clear distinction between archetypes of higher spiritual realms (supraconscious or transpersonal) and those of lower mythological origin. Ken Wilber (1997) has tried to give us a map that integrates the spectrum of consciousness.

Roberto Assagioli designed his map as an egg, which more closely approximates a model of the psyche than the views of Jung or Freud. Instead of the term Higher Self in Assagioli's egg, I like to call it "ME" for "Mediating Experience," which acts as a mediator between the individualized consciousness (ego) and the Universal Spirit. The ME acts as a translator, translating information from the Universal Spirit to the human being. In John 15: 4, it says, "Abide in me, and I in you."

Abide is an old-fashioned word, which means "persevere," "last," "stay with it."

The ME is the nondual consciousness that is personal to each one of us. Stay in me. Stay in the consciousness that mediates between the ego and Universal Spirit. It will communicate to you in a personal way. It can be your partner and friend who will be closer to you than your own breath. Eva Thayer, author of *More We than Me: On Being One with Self and Others* (1985), said she was watching a prayer service in Washington DC after the tragedy of 911 when she heard an internal voice say, "Hear all those prayers being said to God? Who says prayers to Holy Me?" At the time, she was going to church and believed God was out there, not the I AM presence within Me.

ME is my Spirit in microcosm, which is one with the Universal Spirit. It is my nature to be in relationship with the Power greater than myself. This Power responds to and flows out in all directions and multiplies. Faith in this Power activates it. The attributes of God have to become real if I am to become receptive to greater good, abundance, and a sense of well-being. One part of myself (ME) is already in a place beyond fear and confusion, no matter how disturbed my thoughts may be. I must commune with the Infinite Spirit. Imagine all the creative ideas that might spill out if all of me were unified with the Divine Presence, and I truly embodied that truth.

Today all the future is born from our thoughts. The greatest hope we have is the creativeness of our mind, the Spirit of God within us. "There is a power for good, and most certainly we may use It" (1965, 73–74).

Part IV

Applications to the Future

Chapter 18

Spiritual Democracy
and Education

As once the winged energy of delight carried you over
childhood's dark abysses, now beyond your own life
build the great arch of un-imagined bridges.

—Rainer Maria Rilke

More than ever before I am aware that we are both spiritual and communal beings. We are touched by what happens when we interact with others. I ran across a letter, written on February 13, 1982, in my files. After attending the coordinating council kickoff meeting, Bill Aleshire, the assessor and collector of taxes for Travis County, Texas, was moved to write these words to Willie Kocurek, the new chair of Forming the Future:

> I felt you, Mr. K, stretch our perspective beyond the "rice-planting" for today to laying the educational foundation for the mysterious future of our children. And I realized that, for all the concern I have for our children's future, I have taken the remarkable idea of public education for granted.

> It came to me that we parents will, most probably, be alive to witness the beginning and middle of our children's

working careers. What hope could we parents have for the future happiness and success of our children if they were NOT being trained and taught well in a PUBLIC school system? What if the future would belong exclusively to the children of parents who now have the wealth to buy an education for their children independent of the public school system?

You've caused us to consider this.

The practicalities of funding public schools are to be viewed through the social trends of this community. Austinites pay the cost for the growing beauty of this city. With time and continuing trends for new residents to flee our city taxes and increasing congestion, we who remain are faced with the dilemma of wanting to improve the services which make Austin beautiful, but not having the money to pick up the tab by ourselves.

There's so much to consider, this is sort of like a fish trying to eat a sea urchin; you must try many times biting and pulling at the thorny problems before you finally turn it over and get to the substance and the solution to our hunger.

I'm ready to go to work.

—Bill Aleshire

Bill Aleshire worked tirelessly to the very end of the Forming the Future project, serving on his elementary school's school-community leadership team and finally on the executive committee that produced recommendations for restructuring the Austin schools. During the summer of 1982, the executive committee was meeting three nights a week trying to complete the report, and Bill joked "My wife asks me where I'm going and I say 'Forming the Future.' I think I'm married to Forming the Future."

As Bill pointed out in his letter, the issues are thorny ones and the journey is too taxing to make alone. A solitary traveler is likely to quit the road. Finding the way requires a discernment that comes from dialogue in small groups. There is trust and courage that is obtained in pondering deep questions of policy and direction in a group you trust. It is vital that people come together today in groups to consider reinventing education.

This brings us to the concept of spiritual democracy. Frederick Kettner coined the term "spiritual democracy" in 1954 (123). Kettner, a writer, lecturer, and educator, was interested in the education of the deeper nature within human beings. He wanted others to learn about their kinship with the divine. Born in Czernowitz, Austria, in 1886, he received his doctorate in philosophy from the University of Vienna in 1919, then became the chair of ethics at the University of Bucharest.

During World War I, while recuperating in an army hospital, Dr. Kettner began to wonder why there had been over nine hundred wars in what was supposed to be a Christian society? This led him to question the ability of the church to create a peaceful world. He realized a new kind of education was needed to develop the Better or Peace Nature within people. Toward that end, he developed the science of Biosophy, which is derived from two Greek words, *bios*, meaning "life," and *sophia*, meaning "wisdom." *Bios* communicated his quest to express a more abundant life, and *sophia* was the answer to his question "Is there something more than the intellect in man?"

In 1919, Kettner started the first seminar for character education, working the rest of his life to help young people discover a deeper self-knowledge. In 1923, he came to the United States as a lecturer on Spinoza and remained, becoming a citizen in 1930. He loved America deeply and discerned a spiritual undercurrent exemplified by those who had added to its greatness: Franklin, Jefferson, Emerson, Lincoln, Whitman, Margaret Fuller, and others. Kettner believed that the Constitution of the United States was created by beautiful minds because democracy means the people rule.

Kettner felt the traditional churches were not interested fundamentally in peace. By teaching their members that they were sinners and Jesus would save them, the people were not allowed to develop the "image of God" in themselves, and as a result, no inner development took place.

Kettner believed Spirit was within and that human intelligence needed to be liberated.

Spiritual democracy is for individuals who are interested in the spiritual evolution of humankind. The key to this is the development of heart-intelligence. Education should do more than train the young to make a living. It should clarify the mind so that individuals may live in harmony with their souls and with other human beings.

Kettner called for a new education that would emphasize spiritual values and be concerned with the growth of the spirit. He called for these actions:

1. To develop a World Academy of Democracy that would increase the articulation of democracy, create publications, films and other media to analyze world events in relation to the basic issues of democracy and establish a youth movement;
2. To establish an Overall Board of Spiritual Strategy to promote the greater development of spiritual intelligence in cooperation with others, establish centers for character and peace education, create a world fellowship of peace of individuals who can further the growth of democracy and world peace;
3. To create Departments of Peace in the governments of the world;
4. To establish a Peace University in America where individuals would be trained to develop their peace nature;
5. To create Silence Rooms where people could discipline themselves to experience silence and become more creative. The silence rooms would help people become without what they are within.

(Ibid.,152–154)

Dr. Kettner died in 1957 before his vision could be fully implemented, but individuals like Marianne Williamson have joined Congressman Dennis Kucinich in campaigning for the establishment of a Department of Peace at the cabinet level in the United States government, thus carrying on the vision established by Frederick Kettner.

Democracy is a true advance in the evolution of government. In place of rule by a limited few, it brings about the sovereignty of the people.

But sovereignty, without the rule of Spirit, is not enough. The journey of spiritual democracy is to conquer individual greed and selfishness. It requires innate spiritual heroism. There is an excellent model for spiritual democracy within the Native American tradition of the Iroquois that is worth learning about (see chapter 5).

The problem is rooted in the supreme value of scientific materialism held presently by Western civilization. When we learn to see all human beings as souls, not just residents of this state or country, or belonging to this race or that religion, it will be possible to defeat hatred, prejudice, and other destructive emotions. The military must not be the only institution that promises free college education and escape from poverty. At a societal level, we must develop compassionate economics and sustainable economies that create a better way to live for all citizens.

During the 1800s, Transcendentalism was a spiritual and philosophical movement in America. One of the visionary poets from this movement was Walt Whitman who wrote a poem called "Cities of Friends" that promoted the kind of peace envisioned:

Cities of Friends

I dream'd in a dream I saw a city
invincible to the attacks of the whole
of the rest of the earth,
I dream'd that was the new city of Friends,

Nothing was greater than the quality
Of robust love, it led the rest,

It was seen every hour in the actions
of the men of that city,
And in all their looks and words.

—Walt Whitman

Ralph Waldo Emerson wrote about the potentialities of the soul in his essay "Self Reliance." He defined self-reliance as a new respect for the divinity of man, the self as Higher Self, seeing its revolutionary potential we are only now realizing today.

The philosophy of Transcendentalism was derived from the early Quakers of America who believed in transcendent power to transform social and political conditions. They believed in letting conscience be the guide. This worldview of preserving the power of the soul happened just prior to the industrial era. The teachings of the Quakers found their way to Count Leo Tolstoi who, in 1893, was inspired to write *The Kingdom of God Is Within You* (2002), where he laid down his political philosophy of nonviolent resistance.

Tolstoi quoted the voices of Adin Ballou and the abolitionist William Lloyd Garrison, who opposed the system of slavery. *The Kingdom of God Is Within You* captured young Gandhi's interest as an Indian lawyer in South Africa and won him over to follow Tolstoi's influence. Then the philosophy found its way back to its American roots from Gandhi to Martin Luther King and the civil rights movement. Education for spiritual democracy should include educating for nonviolent communication.

Michael Lerner proposes that awe and wonder be the first goals of education:

> Let our teachers be judged on how successful they are at generating students who can respond to the universe, each other, and their own bodies with awe, wonder and radical amazement at the miracles that are daily with us. I don't mean teaching students about awe and wonder as a new subject matter, memorizing facts and passing objective tests . . . Rather, I mean we should teach students to actually embody awe and wonder in the ways that approach their own experience of the universe. Educating for awe and wonder would require a whole new pegagogy. Teaching awe and wonder would not involve teaching a specific religion or specific concept of God in our public schools. The main focus of spiritual education in schools will not be the introduction to other spiritual traditions, but the focus on generating an aliveness to the sacred in students themselves. And the key to that is to have teachers who are alive to the sacred themselves and who

are allowed to see their own creativity and spontaneity to
open this awareness to their students. (Lerner 2000, 247)

The value of teaching mindfulness and spiritual aliveness is to develop
an inner life that can resist totalitarianism in all its subtle forms. It is vital
for students to develop the capacity to maintain their own perspectives
and not allow the community to undermine their own views. They can
then experience what Lerner calls "emancipatory spirituality." This would
include an education for compassion and caring, tolerance and diversity,
citizenship and some of the core streams of knowledge. Lerner believes the
key themes would be the following:

1. The World of Work
2. The Miracle of Body
3. The Meaning of Life
4. Cooperation and Community
5. Birth and Death

The streams would be taught to include much of what is traditionally
taught in science, literature, history, and social sciences. They would not
supplant subjects such as algebra and world history but offer a holistic
curriculum these subjects were intended to provide. Many electives would
be offered on the internet, through distance learning and media kits. The
basic skills of reading, writing, and arithmetic would be mastered by the
sixth grade.

The Dalai Lama has said that "education is in crisis the world over"
(Fox 2006, 7). School districts are interviewing and employing corporate
CEOs and military officers to run the public schools, and not pedagogically
trained individuals. We are in between paradigms. The old paradigms are
not working for the postmodern world.

David Korten says there is a cultural war between a commitment to
Empire and a commitment to the earth community. He writes that the
desire to learn is inherent in our human nature, but schools too often
"serve as institutions for the confinement and test-driven regimentation of
children isolated from the life of community." Hence, Korten says, "It will
fall to today's children to reinvent practically everything" (2006, 350–51).

Supporting children in developing both the basic skills and the required qualities of mind is an essential responsibility of the current adult generation. He writes about 950 college and university presidents who have signed a campus compact to pledge support for students, faculty, and staff to collaborate with their communities in projects that deal with major public issues. Also, a United States–based democracy collaborative involves more than twenty major university research centers, which cooperate in research, teaching, and community action intended to strengthen democracy and civil society locally, nationally, and globally. The vision is that the university will become a resource for democratic citizenship and community service (Ibid., 351–2).

Korten opines that the human mind must be liberated from the idea that there is no alternative to Empire. Korten uses the word *Empire* with a capital *E* as a label for the hierarchical ordering of human relationships based on the principle of domination. "The mentality of Empire embraces material excess for the ruling classes, honors the dominator power of death and violence, denies the feminine principle and suppresses realization of the potentials of human maturity" (Ibid., 20). The growing and organized presence of millions of what Paul Ray calls "cultural and spiritual creatives" can shift the world from a Great Death to a Great Birth to create partnership models, shared learning, and new alliances. Democracy must be practiced through transformative projects such as Forming the Future.

As symbols of transformation, butterflies have always fascinated me. One of the instructors at Wisdom University had pictures drawn of about twenty stages of the metamorphosis of the butterfly. At a class meeting she invited us to pick one of the pictures to symbolize where we were in life at that moment. It was a very powerful discussion. Were we an egg, larva, pupa, or imago—or somewhere in between? Looking at the world today, I believe we are undergoing an acute metamorphosis in which the old paradigm (the caterpillar) has hardened and is now being liquefied and turned into cellular soup. Special islands of pure potentiality are gathering to generate the new forms, the new constellations of creative activity. We must become new humans, the new circles, new communities, the new spiritual democracies. Butterflies teach us not to be afraid of metamorphosis, of transformation.

We are in the midst of an economy that is unraveling because of the depletion of nonrenewable natural resources and the deception of war. The call has been sounded to make a new journey for civilization. We stand at the brink of a new creative opportunity to join the rest of the earth community in liberating ourselves from selfishness.

This will begin with a new form of education both for children and adults. What if educating for awe and wonder became the norm and not just be an after-school program? Can our communities come together to shift what may become a privatized enterprise—the public education of children—before it's too late? Could projects such as Forming the Future start the discussion of values and vision to reinvent the public schools?

The work begins with embracing the truth that we have the capacity to form our future and to make wise choices in the service of the unfolding of Creation.

We do not have to be afraid to heal America. Spirit embraces the idea of unity and wholeness.

Jalal al-Din Rumi's poem, "Prayer Is an Egg," asks us some pointed questions:

Prayer Is an Egg

On Resurrection Day God will say, "What did you do with the strength
and energy your food gave you on earth?
How did you use your eyes?
What did you make with your five senses
while they were dimming and playing out?
I gave you hands and feet
as tools for preparing the ground for planting.
Did you in the health I gave,
do the plowing?"
You will not be able to stand when you hear those questions.
You will end double and finally acknowledge the glory.
God will say, "Lift your head and answer the questions."
Your head will rise a little, then slump again.
"Look at me! Tell what you've done."

You try but you fall back flat as a snake.
"I want every detail. Say!"
Eventually you will be able to get to a sitting position.
"Be plain and clear. I have given you
such gifts. What did you do with them?"
. . .
Then you pray the prayer that is the essence of every ritual:

*God, I have no hope. I am torn to shreds. You
are my first and last and only refuge.*

Don't do daily prayers like a bird pecking, moving its head
up and down. Prayer is an egg.
Hatch out the total helplessness inside.
—Jalal al-Din Rumi, *The Essential Rumi*

Forming the Future, as journey, mythos, and revelation is about hatching out the total helplessness inside and giving away the awesome gifts of God.

Chapter 19

Nudges from the Infinite

It is inclusivity that brings security belonging, not belongings.
—Jeremy Rifkin, "The European Dream: The New Europe Has
Its Own Cultural Vision and It May Be Better Than Ours"

At Wisdom University's Sacred Activism Conference, held in Seattle, Washington, in May 2006, I viewed a PowerPoint presentation given by Paul Ray. One of the slides resonated with me. It was from Ervin Lazlo (see appendix C) and depicts the time we are in now as "Falling into a Hole" with several choices for action: the worst choice is death or attempting to recreate the old level resulting in death; the other choice is to surge forward and create a stable new level. Ray believes we are at a watershed in history where most of the trends of the past are not sustainable. We either rise up to a Wisdom Culture or go down to eco-collapse and the end of an advanced civilization.

Fifty years ago, in America, the culture was divided between moderns and traditionals. Today the moderns comprise 49 percent of the population, the traditionals 24.5 percent, and the cultural creatives 26.1 percent. This last group of people could create a new culture for our time. They are fifty to sixty million people in America and eighty to ninety million people in Western Europe. These are their values: (1) they love nature and are concerned about its destruction; (2) they value relationships and altruism, women's issues and spirituality, the peace and anti-war movements; (3) they are anti-globalization; (4) they reject materialism as just getting and spending; (5) they support social justice and social responsibility; (6) they treasure personal growth; (7) they link the personal and the planetary, the elders and the generations to come.

Paul Ray estimates that cultural creatives make up 45 percent of all voters. They will demand socially responsible alternatives. In the meantime, during this change of eras, which could be very positive, there is a need for resilient communities to buffer against potential shortages and lapses in governmental services.

As I have reflected on Forming the Future as the result of writing this book, I am excited by the possibility of the formation of a new era that allows the solutions to bubble up from the grass roots. Large- and small-scale gatherings of people, together in community, can be held to set intentions for a new wisdom culture. I see this already happening beneath the surface. Vaclav Havel said,

"You too are merely approaching democracy. But you have one great advantage:

You have been approaching democracy uninterruptedly for more than two hundred years" (Vaclav Havel, president of the Czech Republic in an address to the US Congress, February 1990). People are meeting in libraries to discuss how they can have a more sustainable lifestyle or they are joining David Gershon's low-carbon diet to reduce their carbon footprint on the environment.

While antidemocratic forces have risen, at the very same time a more powerful practice of democracy is emerging. Increasingly there are those who are rejecting our unfair economy and igniting a search for a more human-scale and compassionate one. Alarms are sounding about the failure of the public schools and new ideas about remaking them are being imagined. Some schools have realized that democracy is all about change, and change means conflict. Mediation training and conflict resolution are now being recognized as opportunities for students and teachers to learn how to use conflict to bring about school-wide transformation.

Neighborhoods are discovering the power of connectedness to deter violence and enhance peace of mind. Community policing, where police and citizens partner together to reduce crime, is an integral part of the

Hilltop Coalition's block organization structure in Tacoma, Washington. Democracy is not an abstraction but the very essence of fulfillment of the good life and the creation of meaning in community.

Communities will need to be organized around the values of wholeness, spirituality, and wisdom. Many such communities already exist. Frances Moore Lappé (2006, 321–3) suggests that living democracy will require a new language that communicates what is emerging. For example, instead of the word "citizenship," she suggests using "public engagement" or "community engagement"; for the word "activist," she substitutes "engaged citizen" or "empowered citizen"; for "protest and demonstrations," she substitutes "civic obedience," as a positive act to defend democratic values.

Fully realized human beings with all their energy centers activated will become the norm of the new wisdom civilization. Master Stephen Co, a pranic energy healer in the United States, notes there are eleven chakras (energy centers), not seven as is commonly taught (seminar March 28, 2007, Tacoma, Washington). Co said that information about the other four chakras has not been released because untrained novices might damage their internal organs. He showed a diagram of the eleven energy centers, which correspond to the *sepphirot* of the Kabbalah, the Tree of Life. When the energy of life is in balance, there is health in the body, emotions, and mind. "God is energy," he said, reiterating the early spiritual lesson I learned from my first teacher, Uday Mehta. It seems so much more universal to talk about the energy of God than the doctrines about God and to couch it within the Tree of Life.

Human beings who understand spiritual democracy and the importance of community participation will be the norm in a wisdom civilization. An extraordinary Tacoma community leader, Dawn Lucien, described her life in politics to me. She said, "It is amazing that more people are not interested in politics, because every politician makes decisions that affect your life profoundly." Through friendships with key political leaders, she has effectuated significant changes: the restoration of the Union Station Building, the saving of the Murray Morgan Bridge, the funding of the remodeling of the historic Pantages theater, and the resolution of land claims between the City of Tacoma and the Puyallup tribe. Dawn models a life of action regardless of outcome. Failure has never stopped her from acting.

Power means the capacity to act. It converts passive individuals into problem solvers, not blamers. There is power in relationships and in organized numbers. When we got twenty thousand people involved in Forming the Future, we were able to make changes. The turnout of the people was evidence of their commitment to act to make their schools better.

It's ironic that at the age of three I found myself leading people into a hole.

Now seemingly along with the rest of civilization, I have fallen into an "old era" hole. Fortunately, I am aware of some tools to find the way out: (1) sitting in silence; (2) setting intentions; (3) visioning; (4) using the cocreative process; (5) using universal language to describe God and God's presence in, as, and through us; (6) using the power of prayer to shift reality, (7) participating in self-learning communities, and (8) building community participation, using the wisdom of Forming the Future along with other high-technology tools.

There is no "catcher in the rye" waiting to save us from going over the cliff. By giving up the savior myth, we realize we all participate in the process of transformation and getting out of the hole. It's up to us. We are internally wired to access Presence and Universal Intelligence. The more we embody that truth, the faster the trajectory into a Wisdom Civilization. By digging ourselves out from the limiting stories and beliefs we maintain, we gain an invigorated sense of choice about our lives and can be guided by a deepening mystery and mastery. As we share our visions, dreams, and inner messages in communities dedicated to self-learning and transformation, the process of moving forward is much faster.

Future outcomes are unpredictable, but if the moment is right, hope has a generative power. What I thought would involve a hundred people turned out to involve thousands. Sometimes a very small action can set off huge shifts of consciousness and creativity. With so much to be done, we must stay as awake as possible, open at the top to the next nudge from Infinite Spirit. Forming the Future invites us into a breathtaking experience of wisdom and spiritual democracy, the substance of things unseen, our hope of glory.

Whoever you are, no matter how lonely,
the world offers itself to your imagination,
calls to you like the wild geese, harsh and exciting
over and over announcing your place
in the family of things.

—Mary Oliver, from "Wild Geese"

Resources

Small Groups

Artform Conversations is an elegant method that has helped millions of people around the world. It provides objective, reflective, interpretive, and decisional questions. A good paper on the process is available from ICA Associates, Inc. at http://ica-associates.ca.

Center for Conscious Evolution: An online educational connection and communication hub for the global community based on the work of Barbara Marx Hubbard and dedicated to the conscious evolution of humanity and Earth. It is developing plans to support the formation of Evolutionary Learning Communities online and in cities around the world and to offer a framework for greater connection, interaction, and synergy. See http://www.consciousevolution.net.

Co-Intelligence Institute: Founded by Tom Atlee, this is an informative collection on the web of people, processes, and web sites that foster conversations, democracy, and action. See http://www.co-intelligence.org.

Conversation Cafes: These are neighborhood-based, hosted discussions held in public places intended to provide a ninety-minute forum where people of varying views can gather in a safe, relaxed place to explore issues in the world today. See http://www.conversationcafe.org.

Cultural Creatives: Groups are being established around the ideas expressed by sociologist Paul H. Ray and psychologist Sherry Ruth Anderson in their book *The Cultural Creatives: How 50 Million People Are Changing the World*. Their work draws upon thirteen years of survey research studies on over one hundred thousand Americans. New work is funded by Wisdom University to update these findings. See http://www.culturalcreatives.org/invitation.html.

From the Four Directions: Circles have been created all around the world to raise a global voice. Margaret Wheatley is one of the co-founders. See http://www.fromthefourdirections.org.

Gather the Women: Women around the world are feeling a call to show the feminine face of leadership based on principles of harmony, peace, balance, partnership, and cooperation. See http://www.gatherthewomen.org.

Global Consciousness Groups: Duane Elgin and Coleen LeDrew Elgin, who wrote the 1997 report *Global Consciousness Change: Indicators of an Emerging Paradigm,* encourage small groups to study trends in the emerging paradigm. Groups learn to see which actions are most appropriate for the future.
See http://www.awakeningearth.org/reports/gccigcsix.html.

Global Renaissance Alliance (GRA) is to harness the power of nonviolence through a template of prayer, meditation, and deep personal sharing. Based on the work of Marianne Williamson's *The Healing of America*, the GRA offers resources for starting and supporting circles. See http://www.renaissancealliance.org.

Heartland Institute's Thought Leader Gatherings are learning communities for visionaries and change agents. Participants learn a deep form of conversation inside a time-tested format designed to evolve awakened leaders.
See http://www.heartlandinstitute.com and http://www.thought leadergathering.com.

Institute for Noetic Sciences is a nonprofit membership organization that provides local community groups for community building, networking, and collaboration on projects of mutual interest. See http://www.noetics.org.

International Listening Association (ILA) is an organization whose members are dedicated to learning about the impact of listening on human activity. It was formed in 1979 to teach effective listening in all settings. See http://www.listen.org.

New Stories was founded by Bob Stilger to create opportunities for people to discover the new stories in their lives. See http://www.newstories.org.

The Presidio Dialogues: Conversations for Conscious Business was founded by John Renesch whose conversation starters have included Paul Ray, Angeles Arrien, Lynne Twist, Michael Lerner, Matthew Fox, and many others.

These are hosted in San Francisco. See http://www.thepresidio dialogues.org.

Public Conversations Project: Its goal is to foster more inclusive society by promoting constructive conversations among those with differing values, worldviews on divisive public issues. See http://www. publicconversations.org.

Work That Reconnects: Based on the work of activist Joanna Macy, its purpose is to help people uncover innate connections with each other so they may be enlivened to create a sustainable civilization. See http:// www.joannamacy.net.

Conflict Management

The Center for Nonviolent Communication is a global organization that helps people connect compassionately with themselves and one another through nonviolent communication language created by Marshall B. Rosenberg, PhD.

For articles, resources, and training opportunities, go to http://www. envc.org.

Deidre Combs, D. Min. has written a book with the cross-cultural metaphor of the four elements to identify innate conflict personalities. Her book *The Way of Conflict* provides tools, models, resources, and concepts for handling conflict and recognizing styles of conflict. She conducts trainings for such diverse clients as IBM, the Landmine Survivor's Network, and the US Forest Service. See http://www.wayofconflict.com.

Circles

Listening Circles: Inspired by tribal councils of indigenous peoples, sitting in a circle helps people see each other as peers sharing meaning and creativity. A talking stick or object is used to designate the speaker. See Christina Baldwin, *Calling the Circle: The First and Future Culture*. An organization called PeerSpirit has been created by Baldwin and Ann Linnea. Circle practitioners gather groups of people at retreat centers for four-and-a-half days of intensive experiential learning blending council time with training.

See http://www.peerspirit.com.

Sacred Circles for Women offers workshops for women to establish their own spirituality circles. Offers insights into ways to include storytelling, ritual, and discussion. See http://www.sacredcirclesthebook.com.

Sanghas: Thich Nhat Hahn has built a community on the concept of sangha, which includes meditation and social gathering for good. Some are dedicated to issues of importance to community members. They are described in Thich Nhat Hahn's *Friends on the Path*. A large church in Seattle, the Center for Spiritual Living, uses the concept to create small groups around issues of importance to its large community.

Salons: The revival of the French salon has helped create public conversation on a range of subjects in the community. For example, a salon on the topic of "Art and Politics" was held in my home preceded by a short concert by instrumental musicians, then the presentation, a break for wine and hors d'oeuvres, with discussion following. Limited tickets are sold in the salon format to pay for refreshments and to assure enough space is available in the private home. See http://en.wikipedia.org/wiki/salon_ (gathering) and http://www.fordham.edu/halsall/mod/18salons.html.

Wisdom Circles is an organization dedicated to give voice to the values of compassionate community and to make integrity a visible force in the world.

The site offers stories, formats for wisdom circles, and other resources. See http://www.wisdomcircle.org.

World Cafe, a conversation circle invented by Juanita Brown and David Isaacs, focuses on questions that matter. Site offers resources and support for hosting cafes and connecting with others around the world doing similar work. World Cafes are being used in the Cool America campaign to encourage Americans to go on a low-carbon diet initiated by activist, David Gershon. See http://www.theworldcafe.com.

Facilitation Tools

FutureScape™, developed by T. Irene Sanders, is similar to a mind map because it presents information visually as decision-making occurs in the group. The visual record assures people that their ideas are included and help them make connections. Sanders also provides questions for meaningful conversations.

Open Space Technology was developed in the mid-1980s by Harrison Owen. Participants elect a topic or group of their choice and invite others in a large group to join them. Anyone may initiate a conversation, write it on a piece of paper and announce it to the group. The principles of open space technology are (1) whoever comes are the right people; (2) whatever happens is the only thing that could have; (3) whenever it starts is the right time; (4) when it is over, it is over. A book by that title is available written by Harrison Owen, and information is available at http://www. openspaceworld.com/brief_history.htm.

Public Participation: *Public Participation Handbook* by James L. Creighton contains public meeting tools and facilitation advice in a well-formatted text for making better decisions through citizen involvement.

Citywide Initiatives

Imagine Chicago! In 1992, Blisse W. Browne created an organization in Chicago called "Imagine Chicago" to help people imagine and create a positive future for Chicago. It used an appreciative inquiry process citywide, in which fifty at-risk youths interviewed 150-plus community builders in Chicago about the highlights of their lives as citizens and their hopes and plans for the city's future. Initiatives were created that gave its participants a chance to create in more concrete and sustained ways. A book on the project is available at http://www.imaginechicago.org.

Universities

Wisdom University has faculty who teach classes in areas related to this resource file, including Dr. Jim Garrison and Dr. Paul Ray, Institute for the Emerging Wisdom Culture; Deidre Combs, D. Min. on conflict management; Apela Colorado, Indigenous Mind; Jeremy Taylor, dreams and community building, Sacred Activism; Andrew Harvey, Conscious Evolution; Barbara Marx Hubbard, and many others.

Web-Based Resources

Today's leaders can use the internet and other web resources to engage in dialogue and conversation. Some resources include the following:

The Collective Wisdom Initiative explores the field of collective consciousness and includes seed papers, reports on research, and challenging questions. See http://www.collectivewisdominitiative.org.

The Heartland Institute creates Essential Conversations™ for organizations to bring about systemic change. The Heartland Institute assisted Peter Block in creating conversations around the content of his book at a seminar in San Francisco. See http://www.heartlandinstitute.com.

National Coalition for Dialogue and Deliberation brings together groups and individuals to practice and study inclusive, high-quality conversations. Their goal is to elevate the quality of thinking and communication in organizations with a focus on justice, respect, and democracy. See http://thataway.org.

PeerSpirit is an education and service company with an original group process methodology, the PeerSpirit council. A circle is seen as the common root of all cultures, and people accomplish goals through an integrated experience of heart and mind. See http://www.peerspirit.com.

World Initiatives

The web has provided a new tool for democratic participation in such organizations as moveon.org and in reaching people for world initiatives. In addition, the powerful use of the arts through music coupled with conversations and opportunities to increase awareness are ways of creating catalytic movements to seed the grass roots and advocate for change.

Cool America is a new initiative designed to empower communities to go on a low-carbon diet, involves hosting a Global Warming Cafe and mobilizing the political will for change. It includes a "National Day of Climate Action," a call for action on Earth Day, a call at the United Nations World Environment Day for seeking solutions to climate change, and Live Earth concerts worldwide. See http://www.empowermentinstitute.net/lcd.

Process Worldwork was created by Arnold Mindell who brings people and leaders of nations together in large community forums. They are helped with experiential approaches to welcome conflict by dialogue with polarized voices.
Mindell believes everyone is needed to represent reality. See http://www.worldwork.org/home.htm.

<<NOTE TO EDITOR: I would add some updates to this section.>>

Appendix A

SCHOOL-COMMUNITY
LEADERSHIP ASSISTANCE KIT

Introducing The School-Community Leadership Assistance Kit

* About the kit
* Adapt . . . Don't Adopt
* Leadership
* Participation
* Communication

* Hidden Agendas
* Troubleshooting
* Time for Planning
* Planning Assistance

Materials

* About the Kit

The School-Community Planning Assistance Kit is a set of materials that will help local schools participate in the development of a long-range plan for forming the future of your schools.

The kit is designed for use by a local School-Community-Leadership Team, which is broadly representative of community residents, parents, teachers, and community organizations and groups—such as service clubs and neighborhood associations. Though the kit contains materials for step-by-step progress through a planning process, use them selectively and adapt them to meet your needs. The kit has three basic components:

I. CHARTS   Five charts are provided

* Forming the Future outlines how the local planning team fits into the overall district process.
* "Goals for Forming the Future" outlines the objectives of the Forming the Future effort.
* "Goals for School-Community Leadership Teams" outlines specific objectives to be accomplished at the campus level.
* The "Forming the Future Process" outlines stages in the planning process, materials that support each stage, and completion dates.
* A Calendar of Events shows completion dates for each stage.
* A Survey to survey your school community.

II. PLANNING ASSITANCE MATERIALS

These materials—worksheets, checklists, interview summaries, surveys—provide step-by-step direct support for your planning process. They are the tools of the planning team, and there is a set for each planning stage. They are self-explanatory and include process notes to the leaders where necessary. They are intended to be adapted and used as they fit community planning needs. We suggest you put these materials in a three-ring binder for convenient storage and use and adapt the forms as you go along.

III. RESOURCES

Forming the Future staff can assist you in locating materials.

ABOUT FORMING THE FUTURE

Forming the Future is a long-range planning process to study the future facilities, curriculum, and economic needs of the Austin Independent School District over the next ten years. The final product of the project will be to produce a plan for the future that the district staff and community will have shaped.

At the local-campus level, School-Community Leadership Teams will be formed to consider ideas for improving curriculum and facilities that will be economically feasible for the Austin Independent School District to support.

At the district level, a Forming the Future Coordinating Council of citizens will develop plans for improving existing district curriculum and facilities as well as future program requirements that will be economically feasible for the school system to sustain.

The council will review recommendations from each School-Community Leadership Team for inclusion in the Forming the Future plan. It will determine the economic feasibility of all recommendations. The council will conclude its study with a report to the school board on May 10, 1982.

GOALS OF THE FORMING THE
FUTURE PROJECT

The Forming the Future Project will address four general goals that are interrelated and of equal importance:

- To make quality educational programs accessible to all students
- To create schools that will be attractive to all children and their parents

146

- To provide for economic feasibility and to contribute to the financial stability of the school system and the city
- To increase community involvement and support for the schools

GOALS OF THE SCHOOL-COMMUNITY LEADERSHIP TEAMS

School-Community Relations

1. Identify general community concerns about the school.

2. Identify ways to increase the use of community resources at the school.

Curriculum Improvement

3. Identify community priorities for emphasis within existing curriculum at the school.

4. Identify community priorities for additions to the curriculum at the school.

Facilities Improvement

5. Identify community priorities for facilities improvements at the school.

Planning

6. Recommend priorities for district program improvement.

* Information

Information about your school is included in the kit under a separate section labeled "Information."

*Adapt . . . Don't Adopt

You may start in any number of places and go in a number of directions. For example:

- Your school may be in a rapidly growing attendance area with an urgent need for new schools.
- Yours may be an older suburban school with declining enrollment and too much school space. You may be looking to house other community services.
- You may be responding to a threatened or impending cut in funds that may end a successful enrichment program.
- You may be responding to a more general concern about lack of maintenance and operation funds to adequately maintain and repair your building.

Although the same basic planning process will help you address any of these concerns, you will probably have to adapt the planning assistance materials to meet your own needs. You don't have to use them all, either. If some forms are too broad or narrow for your purposes, or if you have already completed certain stages, skip over the forms. They are guides to a practical and logical method of planning. Use the checklist at the end of each stage to be sure you have completed all necessary tasks.

* Leadership

Cooperative school-community planning is a new kind of planning process and requires a new kind of leadership.

Leaders must be committed to the process, not to an end result. They must have the respect and trust of everyone who participates. Because this process is open to all, you will find conflicts of interest and clashes of values. You will find some people will tend to be ignored—because they are known to be troublemakers. And you will find some people expect to carry extra influence—because they are elected officials or because they control resources. Part of the leader's job is to balance participation and decision-making.

You will need a local steering committee to take care of arrangements—printing of forms, newsletters, publicity, arranging for meeting places and refreshments.

*Participation

Cooperative school-community planning requires continued participation by all segments of the community, by residents of all ages and backgrounds, and by members and administrators of community organizations. Each person brings a valuable perspective to the planning process.

Opportunities to participate should be continuous and varied. Although we use the words "leadership team" throughout this kit, membership on the team will fluctuate, and new members should always be welcome. Varied methods of participation will allow people to use their best talents and contribute as fully as they wish. Some people may want to work on specialized task forces, some on the whole planning process, some on a survey. Some people are comfortable in large group meetings, some in small committees, and some in writing reports.

People will own a result only if they've had a hand in creating it all along, and ownership is what cooperative school-community planning is all about.

* Communication

Regular and frequent communication is crucial to the success of this planing process—communication with every reasonable constituency of the public; with community organizations; with the boards of directors, administrators and staff of agencies and governmental bodies; with public media people.

Communication serves two purposes. It is the means for telling people what is happening at each stage and why—for sharing the findings and decisions of the planning team. It is also the means for seeking renewed commitment to the process at each stage. The planning teams needs to check back with the public, parents and community organizations, for confirmation and support in its work throughout the planning process.

* Hidden Agendas

All of us care strongly about certain things and would like results to reflect our desires and goals. All of us will work to see that this happens. If it happens secretly, we say people have "hidden agendas" and are trying to "manipulate" the process or the outcome. The process used in this kit accepts that people will fight for their interest—but they must do so publicly, and they must convince others. Commitment to the process means commitment to the decisions of the entire leadership team. If you want to achieve your "hidden agenda," you must bring it out in the open.

* Troubleshooting

At some point, the planning process may bog down. People may feel the whole thing is collapsing, or failing. If this should happen, stop where you are. Review what you've done so far, step by step. Usually you will find that people interpreted something differently, held conflicting expectations or assumptions, or felt someone "put something over" on them. Once you discover the trouble, clarify it and deal with it to everybody's satisfaction; you will restore good faith, trust, and common understanding. Then you can continue your planning.

* Time for Planning

Once you have browsed through the planning assistance materials, you will discover that the planning process is flexible enough to meet any number of schedules. If you had all the time in the world, a thorough planning job might take two years—it might take a year to get a broad-based commitment to go ahead! On the other hand, if you have a crisis situation that needs to be resolved in six months, you can use the planning materials to get you where you need to be in six months. Do cut corners where you need to. You can compress into one evening's discussion what might also take several weeks of interviews and meetings. What might be accomplished at a more leisurely pace in a series of meetings can be accomplished in a one- or two-day-long intensive sessions. Outside parameters or "givens" may reduce the scope of what you can do. Two important points are the following:

1. The more broadly representative of the entire community your leadership team is, the more safely you can compress time. This is a matter of common sense. You are more likely to reflect the community's feelings, priorities and concerns in a leadership team meeting if the leadership team itself reflects the community. So don't skimp on your first job of getting a broad-based leadership team together.

2. Another key part of the first stage is developing your school-community plan for planning—who is going to do what, how, and by when. Become familiar with the steps in the planning process and look at the deadlines you have to meet. Play around with time schedules, assess your resources, and figure out what corners to cut if necessary. A healthy dose of intelligent common sense will carry you a long way!

(3) Although the principal may serve as chair of the initial meeting, it is wise to let a community member lead the group. You will want to elect a permanent chair at the first meeting. The principal then would serve as an assistant to the chair.

Completion Dates

Each stage has a completion date, and certain information should be submitted to the assistant superintendents.

Here is a listing of due dates and materials to be turned in.
If you have already submitted the information, please disregard.

STAGE 1:   Local-School Level

What: List of members of School-Community Leadership
Team: Who they represent (parent, community leader,
neighborhood organization) and date first meeting was
held. Also submit any nominations from your team for
the Coordinating Council.

Due: November 6

STAGE 2:   Local-School Level

What: Summary of survey of community and additional goals

Due: December 11

STAGE 3:   Local-School Level

What: Priority Needs Summary
Prioritized List of School Plant Improvements

Due: January 15

STAGE 3B: Coordinating Council

What: Identification of District Priorities
Recommendations for Program Improvement

Due: February 12

Stage 1: Get Started

LEADERSHIP NOTES:
First Meeting

I. Welcoming People and Thanking Them for Coming (Principal)

II. Overview of Forming the Future and Its Goals

III. Goals of a School-Community Leadership Team

IV. Are We Representative? Who Else Needs to Be Here?

V. Discussion of Survey/Schedule Survey
   Who Will Summarize Survey Data?

VI. Appointing a Chair of the Team

VII. Tour of School

VIII. Plan for Next Meeting

School Survey

1. What are some things you like about the school?

2. What are some changes you would recommend?

3. What are some things you would add?

4. Do you have any other concerns about the school?

5. What will our students need to know to prepare them for the future?

6. What are the major concerns the School-Community Leadership Team should focus on?

Step 1

Get Started

Step 1 involves beginning. Getting started is not always easy. You must focus on what brings you together, what you hope to accomplish, how, by when, and with whom. Cooperative planning requires that you bring many people into the planning prsocess and that you affirm the importance of accepting differing viewpoints. It is a challenging and rewarding experience you are starting upon.

This step is designed to be used at both the school and district level. It incorporates grassroots participation at both school and district levels. The media should be used to publicize the planning process and to invite participation by interested citizens.

These materials will help you:

- Identify initial ground rules if any.
- Understand the stages in a logical planning process.
- Decide how to expand leadership team membership so that you truly represent the community.
- Understand and explore your feelings about cooperative planning
- Define the problem or concerns you will focus on and the goals you will arrive to reach.

- Chart the process you will use, establishing a schedule for stages and tasks, a plan for keeping communication and participation open, and a means of getting the resources you will need.

Cooperative planning requires that you bring many people into the planning process and affirm the importance of accepting differing viewpoints.

There are two levels of planning occurring simultaneously. First, there will be cooperative planning at the school level with community participation, and there will be cooperative planning at the district level, which includes community participation.

Somebody has to start the process. Sometimes it starts with a small group of people. Sometimes a crisis is impetus for getting together. Or it may be a mandate by the board of trustees to formulate a plan for the future education of children in that district.

Here are some questions to get started:

1. WHO AND WHAT ARE YOU?

School Level: You are a School-Community Leadership Team.
District Level: You are part of the Coordinating Council.

2. WHY ARE YOU HERE?

What are the goals that have brought you together?

3. WHO ELSE SHOULD BE INVOLVED?

Usually at the beginning, not everyone is involved that needs to be. Your planning will be hampered if the needed people do not participate. One of your first steps will be to determine who else to bring in and get involved.

4. WHO TAKES THE LEAD?

At the school level, the principal should initially take the lead, but he/she may wish to appoint a community chairperson as soon as possible.

156

At the district level, a staff person should be assigned to direct the planning process under the jurisdiction of the superintendent. All committee work or Coordinating Council activity should be under a citizen chair, assisted by a staff director.

GOALS

1. To examine the mandate for planning and responsibilities (at both school and district levels)
2. To establish representative planning groups from the community at both school and district levels
3. To hold public meetings and committee or School-Community Leadership Team meetings
4. To involve the media in publicizing the process
5. To explore problems and opportunities
6. To review the planning process
7. To identify "leadership" for the process
8. To complete a plan, identifying publicity and new participants for step 2

EXERCISES

*Where Are We Starting? *Overview of Planning Process *Who Do We Represent? *Who Else Should Be Involved? *How Do We Feel About Cooperative Planning? *Holding a Public Meeting *Defining Our Goals *Our Plan for Planning *What Leadership Do We Need? *Calendar of Events

I. A. WHERE ARE WE STARTING? (School Level)

Use these questions to clarify where you are before your first meeting with the School-Community Leadership Team or Coordinating Council.

1. What are you most concerned about? A brief statement:

2. What are the goals of the School-Community Leadership Team? (Or your Committee?) (See charts.)

3. How does the work of your team fit into the overall district plan?

4. What is your target date for completing what you are to do? How will you report it? (See Calendar of Events and Guidelines for Final Report.)

5. How will you share information and findings to the general public?

Use this form to organize where you are for your first meeting with your Committee or Council.

I. B. WHERE ARE WE STARTING? (District Level)

1. What is the board of trustees most concerned about? (Increased, declining enrollment, improving curriculum, increasing community participation, improving discipline, etc.) A brief statement:

2. What is the mandate of the Coordinating Council? (See charts.)

3. How does the work of the council fit into the overall district plan?

4. What is your target date for completing what you are to do? How will you report it? (See Calendar of Events and Guidelines for Final Report.)

5. How will you share information and findings to the general public?

GENERAL PLAN FOR PLANNING

STEP 1 – GET STARTED

Planning begins with people who share concerns. In stage 1 you'll look at who you are, who else should participate, and what is meant by cooperative planning, and what problems and goals you will deal with during the planning process. You will assemble a broad-based planning team and decide what kind of leadership you need. This stage concludes with the development of your own plan for planning. Then you'll want to publicize the goals of your planning process and seek participation in stage 2.

STEP 2 – GATHER INFORMATION

Here you will gather information about your school and community, organizations that may be part of your solution, and existing resources. Some of the information you'll collect is "hard data," subjective perceptions and feelings about your community. Both types are important, especially when compared against each other.

STEP 3 – IDENTIFY PRIORITY NEEDS

From information in step 2, you will compile a list of needs, some big, some small, some important to many, some important to only a few, some attainable, others "pie in the sky." You will then poll the community, develop criteria, and identify priority needs. These priorities should be communicated to the school community through a PTA meeting or other appropriate event. Make sure you are on target and have the support of your community.

STEP 4 – DEFINE PROGRAM REQUIREMENTS

Stage 4 involves the Coordinating Council in reviewing all campus and district needs. Each priority will be examined in terms of who has the need, why it's not being met, and what is required to meet it. Programs will be designed to meet the needs, proposing staff, equipment, facility and funding requirements and individuals or departments to be responsible for each program. This is done by creating committees to address each area of need including organizations, consultants, educators, and community members to define requirements.

STEP 5 – EXPLORE OPTIONS/DEVELOP PLAN

By now there is a good idea of programs and services that will meet priority student needs and what resources are needed to provide them.

GENERAL PLAN FOR PLANNING (Continued)

Many community people should participate in this stage of generating and evaluating ideas. The organizations identified as major participants—especially those who will be running programs and contributing money or other resources—should participate in evaluating options so the planning group can be sure the final plan suits everybody. You need to test your plan with community people, community organizations, and governing boards and get agreements in principle.

STEP 6 – REFINE PLAN

Now the Coordinating Council assisted by the staff must develop the plan further, develop priorities and estimated budgets. This is the time to make sure the plan is financially sound so that it will have public support. After the plan has been developed by the Coordinating Council, communicate the proposal in public meetings and through written reports to the board of trustees.

STEP 7 – FOLLOW THROUGH

This stage is to be carried out by the Austin Independent School District staff.

At this stage the plan is implemented. Necessary new programs will be developed. Funding sources will be obtained. Administrative structures will be put into place. Procedures for evaluating the plan will be developed. It is important to continue to communicate with the public.

Finally the plan will result in services, programs, and facilities to be used by the students you represent and the people who have participated in Forming the Future.

WHO DO WE REPRESENT?

1. How many of us . . .
    are less than 18 years old? ___
    are 19–35 years old? ___
    are 36–45 years old? ___
    are 46–65 years old? ___
    are over 65? ___

    are women? ___
    are men? ___
    have children living at home? ___
    have children attending public schools? ___
    do not have children living at home? ___

    have paid jobs here? ___
    do not have paid jobs? ___

    have lived here less than 1 year? ___
    have lived here 1–10 years? ___
    have lived here more than 10 years? ___
    do not live here? ___
    plan to live here another 5 years? ___

2. How many of us are representatives of agencies and organized community groups? _____ Name agencies and organizations

3. How many of us are here not as representatives but as interested citizens? _____

Why are we here?

4. Of the representatives, how many of us . . .
   are administrators? ____ are elected? ____
   are board or council members? ____ are hired? ____
   are staff people? ____ volunteer? ____
   are volunteers? ____ are consumers of service? ____
   are appointed? ____
   make policy decisions? _____
   make budget decisions? ____
   make personnel decisions? ____
   do not make decisions, but feel our opinions are sought and are taken seriously? ____

5. Who are we as a group?

6. Does our group represent our community? Can we be effective?

7. Does our group include persons with differing viewpoints who share the concerns we outlined in 1.1?

Who Else Should Be Involved?

Who To Involve

Levels:

1. Know about needs and problems
2. Immediately affected by problems and solutions
3. Use services
4. Have needed resources
5. Have approval power
6. Can give support
7. Have potential to undermine

Community Groups	Level	Who Will Invite?

Agencies

_____

_____

_____

_____

Consumer Groups

_____

_____

_____

_____

Community Groups	Level	Who Will Invite?
_____		
_____		
_____		
_____		

Individuals

_____

_____

_____

_____

_____

_____

_____

_____

_____

_____

LEADERSHIP NOTES:

Do not cut corners in assembling a Leadership Team that truly represents parents, community residents, organizations, and local businesses. Your end result will be only as good as your participants. A well-balanced team will improve your chances of meeting community needs. Your team should never be a closed group. Once you feel you represent your community, it is time to get started.

HOW DO WE FEEL ABOUT COOPERATIVE PLANNING?

Cooperative planning is different from the way we usually plan. Discuss the differences.

TRADITIONAL PLANNING	COOPERATIVE PLANNING
The district involves citizens to review plans that have already been worked out.	The district and citizens develop plans together as joint partners.
The district determines goals and schedules.	The district and citizens jointly determine goals and schedules.

The district has a monopoly on information.	Citizens and district have access to the same information.
Rich schools have more power than poor ones.	Rich and poor schools have equal impact.
There is competition among schools for resources.	Coordination may result in sharing and reducing costs.
The above may lead to duplication or program gaps.	Cooperative planning should lead to better coordination and delivery of services.

HOW DO WE FEEL ABOUT COOPERATIVE PLANNING?

Speaking primarily as . . .
   an agency person _____
   an organization person ____
   a consumer ____
   a private citizen ____
   a parent ____
   a teacher ____

1. I am excited about the following aspects of cooperative planning.

2. My reservations about cooperative planning are

3. I would relax my reservations if

Achieving Consensus

Consensus means a willingness to commit yourselves to a group decision. You will need consensus on problems and goals, priority needs, programs and your final plan. Here are some general pointers for achieving consensus:

1. People need to think about the issues alone and reach personal conclusions. By filling out a form and writing answers to questions, people can focus on their ideas and feelings; reflect a bit. The forms become a personal tool.

2. People need to try out their ideas on others and get reactions. They need to listen to, understand, and react to others' ideas. Small groups of about eight people allow everybody a chance to be heard and to understand each other. Small groups should be mixed so that people are talking with people who may disagree, not just to friends and neighbors whom they know. Any way of dividing them into groups works (such as counting of 1, 2, 3).

3. People need to find a common ground on which they can agree. The real work of finding common ground is done when small groups are required to come up with a consensus report. The talking, convincing, arguing, and compromising take place in the small groups. Asking them to report back to the full group is a check. Chances are good that you will find small group reports converging around some general themes. Those groups that go off on a tangent, or are dominated by a single vocal individual, will

be outweighed by the others. Most large groups feel comfortable with consensus.

4. People need to see consensus emerging. The agreed-upon statement or finding needs to be captured so that everyone knows what is decided. Find a way to write out small group reports so they are visible to all, and don't end a meeting before you have a common statement written down publicly. People trust representatives of their small groups to represent them. If you have a hard time on final large group consensus, if a statement needs to be hammered out, ask for representatives to caucus and let everybody else break for coffee. Reconvene to hear and agree to the final statement worked out by the representatives before closing the meeting.

Defining problems and goals is crucial to your planning. Everything you do in planning will be based on your problem and goal statements. You will check those statements again and again to be sure you are on target.

STAGE 3A: IDENTIFY PRIORITY NEEDS

3.1	**Priority Need**
3.2a	**Community Needs Summary**
3.2b	**Facilities Needs Summary**

STAGE 3B: IDENTIFY PRIORITY DISTRICT NEEDS

(To be provided to each school in January)

Schools will complete the process at stage 3A. The Coordinating Council will proceed through all seven stages.

If you have an idea for program development—an idea for a magnet school, for example—you may wish to request all the planning materials for the remaining stages.

STAGE 4: DEFINE PROGRAM REQUIREMENTS

The committees of the Coordinating Council will determine the program requirements and make recommendations. Each committee has a specific charge and questions to be answered. Each committee will also review the existing goals/programs of the district, the needs assessment data from the schools, and make specific recommendations.

STAGE 5: DEVELOP PLAN

An Executive Committee of twelve to twenty people will do the extensive work to produce a set of priority recommendations for the board of trustees.

STAGE 6: REFINE PLAN

A draft of the plan will be reviewed by SCLTs, school board, parents, teachers, and administrators. In addition, this plan will include proposed facilities and facilities repairs. Hold public hearings for additional input. (See page 27.)

STAGE 7: FOLLOW THROUGH

The Executive Committee has three tasks:

1. Secure commitment to the plan from board of trustees.
2. Hold a bond issue.
3. Establish a monitoring/evaluation process for the plan.

HOLDING A PUBLIC MEETING

Goals of a Public Meeting:

- Make it easy for people to attend

- Let everyone who attends participate
- Accomplish the task for the meeting

Before the Meeting:

1. Select a convenient location.
2. Select a convenient time.
3. Arrange for childcare during meeting.
4. Publicize well ahead of time.
5. Select a room with good acoustics and lighting.
6. Arrange for refreshments to be served.
7. Provide a sign-in sheet with space for name, address, and phone numbers of participants.
8. Invite media coverage.

At the Meeting:

1. Start on time.
2. Be clear about the purpose of the meeting.
3. Announce when the meeting will end and stick to it.
4. Allow everyone to speak on the topic. (Break into small groups if it is a large group.)
5. Keep to the task and the schedule. (If a related topic comes up, jot it down and come back to it.)
6. Be clear about decisions made by consensus. Write them down for everyone to see so that everyone accepts the decision.
7. Accomplish what you set out to do at the meeting.

After the Meeting:

1. Summarize and publicize what happened and what decisions were made.
2. Make summaries available to participants.
3. Follow through on the conclusions of the meeting.

Appendix B

ORGANIZATION OF FORMING THE FUTURE

FORMING THE FUTURE PROJECT

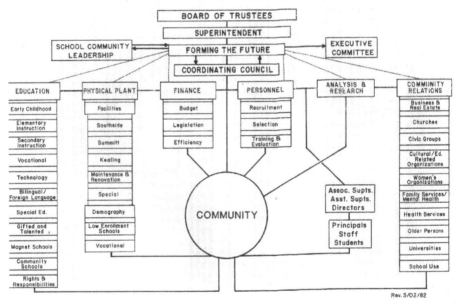

Rev. 3/02/82

Appendix C

ERVIN LAZLO CHART

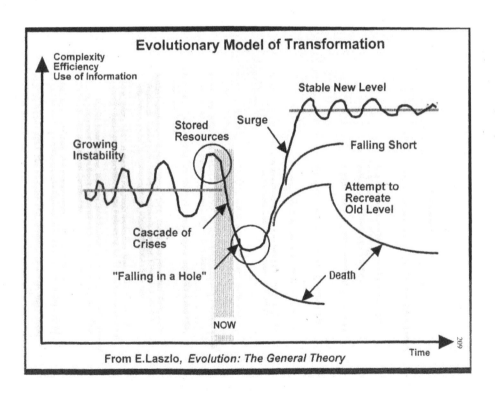

Evolutionary Model of Transformation

From E.Laszlo, *Evolution: The General Theory*

References

Abdullah, Sharif. 1999. *Creating a World That Works for All.* San Francisco: Berrett Koehler Publishers.

Adams, Celeste. n.d. "The Conscious Creation of a New Paradigm: With Dr. William Tiller." *The Spirit of Ma'at* 2, no. 8. Interview. http// www.spiritofmaat.com (accessed February 5, 2007).

Aivanhov, Omraam Mikhael. 1989. *The Fruits of the Tree of Life.* Los Angeles: Prosveta.

Ardagh, Arjuna. 2005. *The Translucent Revolution.* Novato, CA: New World Library.

Armstrong, Karen. 1993. *The History of God.* New York: Alfred A. Knopf.

Arrien, Angeles. 1997. "Shape Shifting the Work Experience." *The New Bottom Line*, edited by John E. Renesch and Bill DeFoore. New York: New Leaders Press.

Assagioli, Roberto. 1965. *Psychosynthesis, a Manual of Principles and Techniques.* New York: The Viking Press.

Atlee, Tom. 2003. *The Tao of Democracy: Using Co-Intelligence to Create a World That Works for All.* Eugene, OR: Co-Intelligence Institute.

Aurobindo, Ghose. 1939. *The Life Divine.* Pondicherry, India: Sri Aurobindo Ashram Press.

Austin Independent School District. 1985. *The Future Revisited: A Progress Report on Forming the Future.* Accessible through ERIC: ED 287896 http://www.eric.ed.gov/sitemap/html_0900000680041ED1.html.

Auvine, Brian. 1981. *A Manual for Group Facilitators.* New York: Center for Conflict Resolution, reprinted by the Fellowship for Intentional Community.

Avery, Michel, Brian Auvine, Barbara Streible, and Lonnie Weiss. 1981. *Building United Judgment: A Handbook for Consensus Decision Making.* New York: Fellowship for Intentional Community.

Avila, Teresa of. 1588. *The Interior Castle.* Glorify His Name! glorifyhisname.com/sys-tmpl/stteresaofavila (accessed February 5, 2007).

Axelrod, Robert. 1984. *The Evolution of Cooperation.* New York: Basic Books.

Baldwin, Christina. 1994. *Calling the Circle.* Newberg, OR: Swan, Raven & Co.

Bernstein, Morey. 1956. *The Search for Bridey Murphy.* London: Hutchinson.

Berry, Thomas. 1999. *The Great Work: Our Way into the Future.* New York: Bell Tower.

Bingham, Frances (Vargas). 1974. A Description of the Implementation and Results of an Early Childhood Verbal Interaction Project. Thesis. University of Texas at Austin.

Bohm, David. 1980. *Wholeness and the Implicate Order.* London, Boston: Routledge & Kegan Paul.

Bolen, Jean Shinoda. 2005. *Urgent Message from Mother: Gather the Women, Save the World.* Boston, MA: Conari Press.

Braden, Gregg. 2006. *The Divine Matrix: Bridging Time, Space, Miracles, and Belief.* Carlsbad, CA: Hay House.

Briggs, Beatrice. 2000. *Introduction to Consensus.* Black Earth, WI: Beatrice Briggs.

Brown, Carolyn T. 2003. *Footprints of the Soul: Uniting Spirit with Action in the World.* Kalamazoo, MI: Fetzer Institute.

Bruteau, Beatrice. 1997. *God's Ecstasy: The Creation of a Self-Creating World.*
New York: Crossroad.

Butler, C. T., and Amy Rothstein. 1987. *On Conflict and Consensus: A Handbook on Formal Consensus Decisionmaking.* Burlington, VT: Food Not Bombs Publishing.

176

Campbell, Joseph. 1949. *Hero with a Thousand Faces*. City: Princeton, NJ: Princeton University Press.

Cochran, Alice Collier. 2004. *Roberta's Rules of Order*. San Francisco, CA: Jossey-Bass.

Combs, Deidre. 2004. *The Way of Conflict*. Novato, CA: New World Library.

Creighton, James L. 2005. *The Public Participation Handbook: Making Better Decisions through Citizen Involvement*. San Francisco, CA: Jossey-Bass.

Csikszentmihaly, Milhaly. 1996. *Creativity*. New York: HarperCollins.

———. *The Evolving Self*. 1993. New York: HarperCollins.

———. *Flow: The Psychology of Optimal Experience*. 1990. New York: Harper Perennial.

Dahl, Robert A. 1989. *Democracy and Its Critics*. New Haven: Yale University Press.

Davies, Paul. 1983. *God and the New Physics*. New York: Simon & Schuster.

———. *The Mind of God*. 1992. New York: Simon & Schuster.

De Tocqueville, Alexis. 1945. *Democracy in America*. New York: Modern Library.

DeFoore, Bill, and John Renesch, eds. 1995. *Rediscovering the Soul of Business*. San Francisco: New Leaders Press.

Dreher, Diane. 1990. *The Tao of Inner Peace*. New York: HarperPerennial.

Dressler, Larry. 2004. *The Consensus Pocket Guide: How to Achieve High-Commitment Decisions*. Boulder, CO: Blue Wing Consulting.

Duffala, Joyce, and Edward Viljoen. 2005. "Spiritual Principles in the Workplace."
Science of Mind 78, no. 2 (February): 30–37.

Eisler, Riane. 2002. *The Power of Partnership*. Novato, CA: New World Library.

Emerson, Ralph Waldo. 1926. *Essays*. New York: Perennial Library Harper Row.

Etzioni, Amitai. 1993. *The Spirit of Community: Rights, Responsibilities and the Communitarian Agenda*. New York: Crown Publishers, Inc.

Feinstein, David, and Stanley Krippner. 1988. *Personal Mythology*. Los Angeles: Jeremy Tarcher.

Firman, John, and Ann Russell. 1994. *Healing the Human Spirit: A Psychosynthesis View of Wounding, Healing and Growth*. Palo Alto, CA: Psychosynthesis Palo Alto.

Fox, Matthew. 2006. *The A.W.E. Project: Reinventing Education, Reinventing the Human*. Saskatoon, SK: Houghton Boston Printers.

———. 1988. *The Coming of the Cosmic Christ*. San Francisco: Harper.

———. 2004. Ernest Holmes, creation spirituality mystic. www.matthewfox.org/recent articles/ (accessed February 5, 2007)

———. 1991. *Creation Spirituality*. San Francisco: HarperCollins.

———, ed. 1982. *Hildegard of Bingen's Books*. Santa Fe: Bear and Company.

———. 1972. *On Becoming a Musical, Mystical Bear*. New York: Paulist Press.

———. 2000. *One River, Many Wells: Wisdom Springing from Global Faiths*.
New York: Tarcher/Putnam.

———. 1983. *Original Blessing*. Santa Fe: Bear & Company.

———. 1984. *The Reinvention of Work: A New Vision of Livelihood for Our Time*. San Francisco: Harper.

Gardner, Howard. 1991. *The Unschooled Mind: How Children Think and How Schools Should Teach*. New York: BasicBooks.

Gardner, Howard, and Emma Laskin. 1995. *Leading Minds: An Anatomy of Leadership*. New York: Basic Books.

Gastil, John. 1993. *Democracy in Small Groups: Participation, Decision Making, and Communication*. New York: New Society Publishers.

Gesell, Izzy. 1997. *Playing Along: 37 Group Learning Activities Borrowed from Improvisational Theater*. Northhampton, MA: Whole Person Associates.

Goldsmith, Joel S. 1962. *Our Spiritual Resources*. New York: Harper/ Collins.

Goswami, Amit. 2001. *Physics of the Soul*. Charlottesville, VA: Hampton Roads.

———. 1992. *The Self-Aware Universe: How Consciousness Creates the Material World*. New York: Tarcher/Putnam.

Graymont, Barbara. 1972. *The Iroquois in the American Revolution*. Syracuse, NY: Syracuse University Press.

Green, Brian. 2000. *The Elegant Universe*. London and Sidney: Random House/Vintage.

Grinde, Donald A. 1977. *The Iroquois and the Founding of the American Nation*.

San Francisco: The Indian Historian Press.

———, and Bruce E. Johansen. 1995. *Exemplar of Liberty: Native America and the Evolution of Democracy*. Los Angeles: American Indian Studies Center.

Grof, Stanislav. 1990. *The Holotropic Mind*. San Francisco: HarperSanFrancisco.

———. n.d. Ken Wilbur's Spectrum Psychology.

http://primal-page.com/grofken.htm (accessed February 5, 2007)

Hahn, Thich Nhat. 2002. *Friends on the Path: Living Spiritual Communities*.

Berkeley, CA: Parallax Press.

———. 1992. *Peace Is Every Step: The Path of Mindfulness in Everyday Life*. Berkeley, CA: Parallax Press.

———. 1992. *Touching Peace: The Art of Mindful Living*. Berkeley, CA: Parallax Press.

Hall, Gene E., and Shirley M. Hord. 1987. *Change in Schools: Facilitating the Process*. Albany, NY: State University Press.

Hart, Betty, and Todd Risley. 2003. "The Early Catastrophe: The 30 Million Gap."

American Educator (Spring).

Hawkins, David. 1995. *Power v. Force: An Anatomy of Consciousness*. Carlsbad, CA: Hay House.

Hay, Louise. year. *You Can Heal Your Life*. Carlsbad, CA: Hay House, Inc.

Hillman, James. 1989. *A Blue Fire: Selected Writings by James Hillman*. Ed.

Thomas Moore. New York: Harper and Row.

Hock, Dee. 1999. *Birth of the Chaordic Age.* San Francisco: Berrett-Koehler.

Hoeller, Stephan A. 2002. *Gnosticism: New Light on the Ancient Tradition of Inner Knowing.* Wheaton, IL: Quest Books.

Holmes, Ernest. 1919. *Creative Mind and Success.* New York: G. P. Putnam's Sons.

———. 2001. *Love and Law.* Ed. Marilyn Leo. New York: Jeremy Tarcher/Putnam.

———. 1965. *The Power of an Idea.* Edited by Willis Kinnear. Los Angeles: Science of Mind Publications.

———. 1926. *The Science of Mind.* New York: G. P. Putnam's Sons, 1926.

———. 2007. "A Spiritual Universe." *Science of Mind* 80, no. 4 (April). (Excerpt from Holmes's last public address, "You are a Wonderful Person," given February 14, 1960).

———. 1943. *This Thing Called Life.* New York: G. P. Putnam's Sons.

———. n.d. What We Believe. On United Church of Religious Science web site. http://www.religiousscience.org/ucrs_site/philosophy/believe.html (accessed February 5, 2007).

Houston, Jean. 1995. *Manual for the Peacemaker: An Iroquois Legend to Heal Self and Society.* Wheaton, IL: Quest Books.

———. 1982. *The Possible Human.* Los Angeles: J. P. Tarcher, Inc.

Hunter, Dale, Anne Bailey, and Bill Taylor. 2001. *The Art of Facilitation: How to Create Group Synergy.* New York: Fisher Books.

Iacofono, Daniel. 2001. *Meeting of the Minds: A Guide to Successful Meeting Facilitation.* Berkeley, CA: MIG Communications.

Jacobi, Jolande, ed. 1978 *C. G. Jung: Psychological Reflections, A New Anthology of His Writings.* New York: Princeton University Press.

James, William. 1902. *The Varieties of Religious Experience.* New York: Longmans, Green & Co.

Jantsch, Erich. 1980 *The Self-Organizing Universe: Scientific and Human Implications of the Emerging Paradigm of Evolution.* New York: Pergamon.

Juline, Kathy. 1996. An interview with Rev. Doctor Michael Bernard Beckwith.
Science of Mind 89, no. 12 (December).

Kaner, Sam. 1996. *Facilitator's Guide to Participatory Decision-Making.* New York: Community at Work.

Keck, L. Robert. 1992. *Sacred Eyes.* Boulder, CO: Synergy Associates, Inc.

Kelsey, Dee, and Pam Plumb. 1997. *Great Meetings! Great Results.* New York: Hanson Park Press.

Kettner, Frederick. 1954. *Biosophy and Spiritual Democracy: A Basis for World Peace.* New York: Vantage Press.

Kocurek, Willie. 2000. *The Wit and Wisdom of Willie Kocurek.* With Ramona Van Loan. Austin, TX: Eakin Press.

Korten, David C. 2006. *The Great Turning: From Empire to Earth Community.*
Bloomfield, CT: Kumarian Press.

Kozol, Jonathan. 1992. *Savage Inequalities: Children in America's Schools.* New York: Harper & Row.

Lappé, Frances Moore. 2006. *Democracy's Edge: Choosing to Save Our Country by Bringing Democracy to Life.* San Francisco, CA: Jossey-Bass.

Leach, Shari. 2004. *Head, Heart & Hands: Lessons in Community Building.*
Boulder, CO: Wonderland Hill Development Company.

Lerner, Michael. 2000. *Spirit Matters.* Charlottesville, VA: Hampton Roads Publishing Company, Inc.

Leu, Lucy. 2003. *Nonviolent Communication Companion Workbook: A Practical Guide for Individual, Group or Classroom Study.* Encinitas, CA: PuddleDancer Press.

Levoy, Gregg. 1997. *Callings: Finding and Following an Authentic Life.* New York: Three Rivers Press.

Liechty, Daniel, ed. 2005. *The Ernest Becker Reader.* Seattle, WA: University of Washington Press.

Lynch, Thomas D. and Cynthia E. 1998. *The Word of the Light.* Baton Rouge, LA: Hara Publishing.

Mann, Barbara A., and Jerry L. Fields. 1997. "A Sign in the Sky: Dating the League of the Haudenasaunee." *American Indian Culture and Research Journal* 21, no. 2.

Marion, Jim. 2000. *Putting on the Mind of Christ*. Charlottesville, VA: Hampton Roads Publisher.

McGregor, Douglas. 1960. *The Human Side of Enterprise*. New York: McGraw-Hill.

McTaggart, Lynne. 2001. *The Field: The Quest for the Secret Force of the Universe*. London: Harper Collins.

Mindell, Arnold. 1992. *The Leader as a Martial Artist: An Introduction to Deep Democracy, Techniques and Strategies for Resolving Conflict and Creating Community*. San Francisco: HarperCollins.

———. 1995. *Sitting in the Fire: Large Group Transformation Using Conflict and Diversity*. Portland, OR: Lao Tse Press.

Moore, Thomas. 1992. *Care of the Soul*. New York: HarperCollins.

Murdoch, Maureen. 1990. *The Heroine's Journey*. Boston: Shambhala.

National Diffusion Network. n.d. *Educational Programs That Work*. http://www.ed.gov/pubs/EPTW/index.html (accessed February 5, 2007).

Needleman, Jacob. 2003. *Two Dreams of America*. Kalamazoo, MI: Fetzer Institute.

O'Murchu, Diarmid. 2002. *Evolutionary Faith*. Maryknoll, NY: Orbis Books.

Owen, Harrison. 1992. *Open Space Technology: A User's Guide*. Potomac, MD: Abbott.

Pagels, Elaine. 1978. *The Gnostic Gospels*. New York: Random House.

Papegaaij, Bard and Michal. n.d. "The Human Who Is Not a Resource—Will Your Company Survive the Next 20 Years." On Workplace Spirituality web site. http://www.workplacespirituality.info/HumanNotResource. html (accessed February 5, 2007).

Peck, M. Scott. 1987. *A Different Drum: Community Making and Peace*. New York: Simon and Schuster.

Prigogyne, Ilya, and Isabelle Stengers. 1984. *Order Out of Chaos: Man's New Dialogue with Nature*. New York: Bantam Books.

Ray, Paul, and Sherry Ruth Anderson. 2000. *The Cultural Creatives*. New York: Harmony Books.

Richardson, Peter Tufts. 1996. *Four Spiritualities*. Palo Alto, CA: Davies-Block Publishers.

Rilke, Rainer Maria. 1981. *The Selected Poems of Rainer Maria Rilke*. Trans.

Robert Bly. New York: HarperCollins Publishers, Inc.

Rosenberg, Marshall. 1999. *Nonviolent Communication . . . A Language of Compassion*. New York: Center for Nonviolent Communication.

Rumi, Jalal al-Din. 1995. *The Essential Rumi*. Trans. Coleman Barks with John Moyne. New York: Harper.

Sahtouris, Elisabet. 1996. *Earth-Dance: Living Systems in Evolution*. Alameda, CA: Metalog Books.

Saint, Steven, and James Lawson. 1994. *Rules for Reaching Consensus*. New York: Pfeiffer & Company.

Salinger, J. D. 1951. *The Catcher in the Rye*. Boston: Little, Brown & Co.

Scovell Shinn, Florence. 1941. *Your Word Is Your Wand*. Brooklyn, NY: Gerald R. Ricard Publishers.

Schwartz, Stephan A. 1978. *The Secret Vaults of Time*. New York: Grosset & Dunlap.

Senge, Peter. 1990. *The Fifth Discipline*. New York: Doubleday Currency.

———, C. Otto Scharmeir, Joseph Jaworski, and Betty Sue Flowers. 2005.

Presence. New York: Doubleday Currency.

Shaffer, Carolyn, and Kristin Anundsen. 1993. *Creating Community Anywhere: Finding Support and Connection in a Fragmented World*. New York: J. P.

Tarcher.

Sheldrake, Rupert. 1981. *A New Science of Life: The Hypothesis of Formative Causation*. London: Blond and Briggs.

———. 1988. *The Presence of the Past*. London: Collins.

———. 1991. *The Rebirth of Nature*. London: Collins.

Smith, Huston. 1976. *Forgotten Truth*. San Francisco: Harper.

Spady, Richard J., and Richard S. Kirby. 2002. *The Leadership of Civilization Building*. Seattle, WA: Forum Foundation.

Stauffer, Edith. 1987. *Unconditional Love and Forgiveness*. Whittier, CA: Triangle Publishers.

Swimme, Brian, and Thomas Berry. 1992. *The Universe Story*. San Francisco: Harper Books.

Talbot, Michael. 1991. *The Holographic Universe*. New York: Harper Perennial.

Taylor, Jeremy. 1983. *Dreamwork*. New York: Paulist Press.

———. 1998. *The Living Labyrinth*. New York: Paulist Press.

Teilhard de Chardin, Pierre. 1964. *The Future of Man*. London: Collins.

———. 1959. *The Phenomenon of Man*. New York: Harper Brothers.

Thayer, Eva. 1985. *More We Than Me: On Being One with Self and Others*. San Antonio: TES Publishing Company.

Tiller, William. n.d. In "How the Power of Attention Alters Matter." *Spirit of Ma'at*.

http://www.spiritofmaat.com (accessed February 5, 2007).

———, Walter Dibble, and Michael Kohane. 2001. *Conscious Acts of Creation: The Emergence of a New Physics*. Walnut Creek, CA: Pavior Publishing.

Tolstoi, Leo. 2002. *The Kingdom of God Is Within You*. Lincoln Nebraska: University of Nebraska Press.

Troward, Thomas. 1904. *The Edinburgh and Dore Lectures*. New York: New Thought Heritage Books.

———. 1917. *The Law and the Word*. New York: R. M. McBride and Co. Underwood, Paula Spencer. 1997. *Franklin Listens When I Speak*. San Anselmo, CA: Tribe of Two Press Publishing.

———. 1993. *The Walking People, a Native American Oral History*. San Anselmo, CA: Tribe of Two Press Publishing.

———. 1983. *Who Speaks for Wolf?* Bayfield, CO: Tribe of Two Press Publishing.

———, and Rita Reynolds Gibbs. 1984. *Who Speaks for Wolf Teacher's Guide*.

Austin, TX: Meredith Slobod Crist Memorial Fund.

Vaughan, Frances. 1985. *The Inward Arc*. New York: New Science Library.

Wheatley, Margaret J. 1992. *Leadership and the New Science*. San Francisco: Berret-Koehler.

Whitehead, Alfred North. 1978. *Process and Reality*. Omaha, NE: University of Nebraska Press.

Whyte, David. 1994. *The Heart Aroused: Poetry and the Preservation of the Soul in Corporate America*. New York: Doubleday.

Wilber, Ken. 1997. *The Eye of Spirit: An Integral Vision for a World Gone Slightly Mad*. Boston: Shambhala.

Wilcox, David. n.d. *Guide to Effective Participation*. On Partnerships Online.
http://www.partnerships.org.uk (accessed February 5, 2007).

Williamson, Marianne. 1997. *The Healing of America*. New York: Simon & Schuster.

———. 1992. *Return to Love*. New York: Harper Collins.

Wolf, Fred Allen. 1999. *The Spiritual Universe*. Portsmouth, NH: Moment Point Press.

Young, Arthur. 1976. *The Reflexive Universe*. Lake Oswego, OR: Robert Briggs Associates.